SMASHING DECEPTION
IN THE HOUSE OF GOD
{Expanded Edition }

SHANE W ROESSIGER

Copyright © 2016 by Shane W Roessiger

First Edition – 2013

Expanded Edition - 2016

All rights reserved

Cover Illustrated by Ollie Pengilley

Revised by Elaine A Powers

ISBN: 1536976156

13-ISBN: 9781536976151

Printed in the United States of America

H.O.T. House of Truth

Revelation 3:15-18

Not cold. Not lukewarm. Be H.O.T.

Nokomis/Florida-USA

www.hothouseoftruth.com

DEDICATION

First and foremost, I dedicate this book back to the Holy Spirit, my comforter, my guide, and the One who inspired me from cover to cover. Without Him, I could do nothing. So this book is His. I'm just a steward of His Truth, His revelations. I thank Him for choosing me first.

Secondly, I want to thank my wife, Marlene, my other half, for her Godly influences and always keeping me on track. Thank you, Baby, for loving me and loving Christ in me.

I want to thank my mother and father for loving me when I did not love myself, loving me through my incarcerations, heavy drug use, and being a terror sometimes. Love never fails. Thank you, Herbert & Linda Roessiger. I love you! Always.

I want to thank Steve and Elaine Powers; Steve first for lending his wife as she spent many hours revising this book over and over. Thank you, Elaine, you are the best, and God is going to shock you.

Finally, I thank everyone else in our H.O.T. Family. You guys rock. Thank you for your support in every way. Love, Shane

ABOUT THE AUTHOR

I never met a man who sees ahead of his time, just as in the days of old; a man whose tongue is the pen of a ready writer; a man, in whom the fire is shut up in his bones, burning day and night. I never met a man whose zeal and love for the uncompromised Truth consumes, compels, and provokes. I never met a man willing to live and to die for what he believes; I never met a man who would love a woman just as Christ loves the Church, until I met Shane, my husband.

Baby, may grace abound in you so that you can always do what you are fully committed to do until He returns: **"And Micaiah said, As the LORD liveth, what the LORD saith unto me, that will I speak. "1 Kings 22:14**

Having done all with tears and joy, we will stand strong before our Father, holding hands, as one, just as it was from the beginning.

Eu te amo,

Marlene Roessiger

TABLE OF CONTENTS

FOREWORD BY THE BODY OF CHRIST

"I've been moaning & groaning and asking myself, "Where Has The Gospel Gone?" Thank you and God Bless You" Laverne Blake-Brown

"Truly spoken like a Shane, a man of God, who loves to see God's people free and doing exploits." Jonathan Keener

"Blow the trumpet in Zion, and sound an alarm in My Holy mountain! Let all the inhabitants of the land tremble; For the day of the Lord is coming...See more for it is at hand"! (Joel 2:1). More fire on you, Brother, in Jesus' name!" Dominic Vitale

"On time...in line...yes...He is cleaning and purging and bringing His bride into alignment!" Jacqueline McMillen

"Oh God, forgive us. Release your fire upon your people. Rise up, O Holy Spirit, within us. Rise up, O fire of God. Give us a heart for the harvest. Give us a deep desire to press into all that you have for us. Rise up, O Lord. To you and you alone belongs all the Glory. Thank so much...on time." Armstead Williams Vickie

"Thank for this word, my brother! I pray that everyone you sent this to has the ears to hear, like I did! I pray that their hearts are as appreciative as I am! False prophets are out to be exposed! Thanks again!" Shari Nelson

"Shane, the Lord has put so much lately in my thoughts regarding the "institutional church" vs. us actually being "the church" and His Bride. I am so fed up with religiosity and what people call church, and I'm seeking God with all my heart....and He is revealing the word to me in greater ways than ever before. Thank you for being real. I also believe if Jesus came back to cleanse the temple he would start with the pulpit in many churches, sad to say. Keep sounding the alarm, Brother!" Susie Craft

"That was good. Don't ever apologize when God gives you a word, just be obedient. A prophet is never loved by all since he is that watchman on the wall, sometimes blowing judgment, truth, or encouragement. Be blessed." Mary Merth

"Yes, yes, truth, truth!! Few there are who find it. The REMNANT is rising!" Kayce Spiegelberg Gilcrist

H.O.T. HOUSE OF TRUTH

INTRODUCTION

A WORD FROM MARLENE ROESSIGER

No truth should be spoken without mercy. My prayer is that we, as writers, and you, as a reader, will handle the truth found in this book in the way that pleases the Father: righteously...Let these pages be a place where mercy and truth will meet together...

"Let not mercy and truth forsake you; Bind them around your neck; Write them on the tablet of your heart." Proverbs 3:3

A WORD FROM SHANE ROESSIGER

We are a body of believers – the Church. We must take a look at our present day status. We must go to our brother and pull him out of the pit. Oh, you think I am talking about the lost? No, I'm talking about you, Brother. We think that we go to church and that we are fine. You have not made it yet, and neither have I. Let's take a look at some present day truths. Let's look at the Bible with a prophetic eye. I am called to the church. God will use the foolish to confound the wise. I am writing this book under the inspiration of the Holy Ghost - the same Holy Ghost that was with Paul is with me. I also write it out of obedience. We have a foundation laid. We have God's word, and everything said in this book, it is in the Bible. I encourage you to check what I say with the Word. God has not stopped talking to His people. He is alive. He is with me. This Bible is what is called a sword. Swords, do they kill? The Word is designed to kill your flesh. The Word of God is a sword. Do you agree? It is not just to fight the Devil. It is to stab yourself – your old man. This is legal suicide in the Kingdom. Friend, our high calling, the big call, is to die to ourselves. This is the only legal suicide in the Kingdom of God. When I speak, I speak on His behalf - under the inspiration of the Holy Ghost – I need to make that clear. Some people do speak on their own behalf, so please test every word I say with the word of God, the unadulterated word, not a remix, not a word that has been unsharpened through the hands of man. Stick to the King James Version – that is my best opinion.

The Word of God is written to guide us into a Godly life, to instruct us, just as a loving Father would do.

A WORD TO THE CHURCH

BLACK & WHITE

"The Black & the White are significant for My house. No more compromising. This is how I see things. So shall My people whom I shall call out from among them. It's not about man. I will pour out this new wine upon those who have the new skin. I will destroy every little fox. Those who have become like Eli and could not hear My voice and let these compromising things to go on in My house, they will spiritually perish and will cause My glory to be lifted. I am raising up these men and women in this day. They will obey Me rather than man. They will be men and women who know the difference between good and God."

"In this coming season, I will reveal those who are using my church for their own gain, those who have used my words to entice my sheep, who have let go of what I have given them for their own gain. For I have given time for repentance and found no repentance. I am cleaning house. Some will be publicly exposed. Some ministries will come to not silently. Losing what they hold so precious, they will repent. I am doing this because I love them. They will not perish into everlasting fire, away from me."

"Perverse disputing of men of corrupt minds, and destitute of the truth, supposing that gain is godliness: from such withdraw thyself. But godliness with contentment is great gain. For we brought nothing into this world, and it is certain we can carry nothing out and having food and raiment let us be therewith content. But they that will be rich fall into temptation and a snare, and into many foolish and hurtful lusts, which drown men in destruction and perdition. For the love of money is the root of all evil: which while some coveted after, they have erred from the faith, and pierced themselves through with many sorrows. But thou, O man of God, flee these things; and follow after righteousness, godliness, faith, love, patience, meekness. Fight the good fight of faith, lay hold on eternal life, where to thou art also called, and hast professed a good profession before many witnesses." 1 Timothy 6:5-12

Church, arise and shine. Now order is coming back to the Body. Not the order that religion tries to put on you. This kind will be dismantled. This kind is disorder. This reformation will bring a divine order. Not a man-made hierarchy but a Body full of all members and parts that restore this lack of order back to order so as to breakdown the man-made foundation. No more man-made institution, but pure faith and God moving among us all, to all, for all, through all.

We are in the building process, and the foundation is set. It is Christ. We will not build upon ideas and programs. We are going to build on the power of the cross and the blood that sets us free. His Word is truth, and this is His house. We are His hands, and we are about to overtake every obstacle we come across. We are seeing God's hands move and His plan, His blueprints, being manifested in this region. We will not follow a denomination. We will not get it from a successful pastor. We will not build on any man made foundation but on the Rock. This house shall stand the test of time. His glory will fill this place; His truth will go around the world from here and there to everywhere. Don't say no. Yes, He can! Gideon did it! Are you ready?

God is shaking everything that can be shaken. Every man-made, compromising ministry will fall. Testing time is here just as in the days of old. We will see God be God and His enemies will be scattered. We will not make alliances with the world. Revival is here. His power is here. He is here. Get ready, get ready. It's time to take this thing to another level. We are not going to play church. We are going to be changed from glory to glory.

God is preparing a bride, not a harlot. We are His. The same God that created everything will marry us to Himself, and we will be like Him forever. Amazing! Think about it. We will be like Him, and we will be with Him forever.

In this passage, **Mathew 7:24-27**, you see Jesus talking about people who are already saved or ones who think they are saved. Go on and find out. They are going to be rejected.

"Therefore whosoever heareth these sayings of mine, and doeth them, I will liken him unto a wise man, which built his house upon a rock: And the rain descended, and the floods came, and the winds blew, and beat upon that house; and it fell not: for it was founded upon a rock. And every one that heareth these sayings of mine, and doeth them not, shall be likened unto a foolish man, which built his house upon the sand: And the rain descended, and the floods came, and the winds blew, and beat upon that house; and it fell: and great was the fall of it." Matthew 7:24-27

"And why call ye me, Lord, Lord, and do not the things which I say? Whosoever cometh to me, and heareth my sayings, and doeth them, I will shew you to whom he is like: He is like a man which built an house, and digged deep, and laid the foundation on a rock: and when the flood arose, the stream beat vehemently upon that house, and could not shake it: for it was founded upon a rock. But he that heareth, and doeth not, is like a man that without a foundation built an house upon the earth; against which the stream did beat vehemently, and immediately it fell; and the ruin of that house was great."

Luke 6:46-49

What you read in **Luke 6:46-49** is what I'm seeing and prophesying about. Man-made is created from the dust. It is sand. Jesus is the rock – His word is bread. There is coming a financial crisis, food crisis, and tribulation, but every house built on the rock – JESUS – will withstand any storm. Those ministries and denominations that do things the way they want and operate out of the flesh are going to come down. It's in the Word. **Mathew 24** is a chapter in the Bible that gives us a glimpse of what is to come. We are being prepared just as Noah was prepared. This is why God is shaking His beloved and going to use His prophets to bring forth truth. Look around - playtime is over. The harvest is ready.

Are you ready? God is saying, "Become a soul winner (Prov 11:30)." We sing, "Do what You will," but we are doing what we want. Become true worshippers. We are that pearl of great price. He paid for us in full when He sent His son. God is trying to mobilize His kingdom. No better sacrifice could you bring to Him. No amount of money could you give that can compare to bringing a soul to Him in every service. God didn't say, "He who goes to church is wise," but, "He who wins souls is wise." We, as a Body, need to stop playing church and become THE church. What you do in secret for the Lord will be rewarded in the open. Favor will be on you like a coat, and you will feel complete, like fruit that just happens. It is such a joy to be part of the Master's plan. Let's activate the Body of Christ. Are you really ready?

"For this wind, **the wind of change,** changes your mind, changes your desires, changes your focus, changes your unbelief, and changes your rituals. **Put your wings up**, ride this wind of change. Don't let this wind knock you down. **Ride it and change into my image**, says the Lord."

Word released on May 11th, 2008

GATES

This book is written to open the eyes of the blind. We have allowed the enemy to deceive and bewitch us and even to minister to the soul. We are not called to be soulish ministers but to minister to the spirit of men! We think that everything is glorious. Everything is great. God has news for you: It is not, but it will be when He gets finished! He said, "I will build my church and the gates of hell will not prevail (**Matthews 16:18**)." Let us not be entangled in the affairs of Babylon (**Revelation 18:3**).* Many will tell you different things, but here are the Words of life: This book of the law shall not depart out of your mouth (**Joshua 1:8**).

Do you see? We have Baal worship in God's house. We have Jezebel controlling leadership. We have people depending on Babylon (on the World system) and not on Jehovah Jirah. Do you realize that people are waiting for the falling away, not even knowing that buildings all over the world on Sunday morning are full of people in apostasy?

Apostasy is about the heart. Do you realize that when you allow pagan worship and celebrations and traditions, when you allow yourself to enjoy their delicacies, you are allowing their gods to have access into your family, your finances, and your life? Do you not yet know that God has said, "Come out of the harlot, Babylon? (**Revelation 18:4**)." Do you realize that Babylon is in our churches? Do you think that all the blood, sweat, and tears that God's prophets wrote to us about this are just good ideas? Do you know that Jesus isn't just talking smack in **Revelation chapter 2 and chapter 3?**

We must close the gates of our fellowships, our homes, and our lives. Do you know that the church is full of Baal's prophets, covering leaders and pimping God's children?

Jesus said, "Give up this life." We hear, "Everyday can be a Friday." Wow! Friday is payday! All these are doctrines of Baal (of the flesh) under the Anti-Christ government that are in the church. So every little god has a face, such as Dagon, a fertility god. When the Bible talks about His house, He is talking about idol worship, such as perversion, running rampant. When we watch or agree, we are worshipping Baal - the lord of flies, Satan himself and all his demons. God spoke through the apostle Paul about Satan turning himself into a messenger of righteousness (**2 Corinthians 11:14**). We must test the spirits, but how can we if the world is in us more than God?

Do you not see a powerless, bound up church with a fancy building, beautiful stain glass windows, and latte machines, just like the church of Laodicea? This book will open our eyes. Only the Truth will set us free. Remember when Solomon allowed all the other gods to mix with his? These are shadows of today's reality. Present day truth. Can you handle the truth? You must. We really have no choice. Either we follow truth or we become deceived.

Lots of folks, when they are approached with the truth, deny it. They get offended. Remember: Jesus is the rock of offense. You see. There is no formula. It's like this: Speak the truth. See truth. Hear truth. Repent. If you are being convicted or involved in offense, then break agreement with it. Walk away from it. There is nothing new under the sun. It just has a new name, a new face, to go along with the times. There are only two kingdoms: God's is the kingdom of light and the other is Satan's, the kingdom of darkness. Unfortunately, we have mixed the two in the Body of Christ. Jesus is warning us now.

What is happening when idolatry is no longer wrong? Let's read: **"Woe unto them that call evil good, and good evil; that put darkness for light, and light for darkness; that put bitter for sweet, and sweet for bitter!" Isaiah 5:20**

All through the Old Testament, God was very adamant that we do not mix seed, but Satan has seed in all the church. We know the Bible says that the enemy has done this. It's called tares. God's fire is about to burn up all the corruptible seed by His light!

A pure bride, a holy nation, a spotless one washed in the blood will emerge! It will rise up!

"Through the tender mercy of our God; whereby the dayspring from on high hath visited us, To give light to them that sit in darkness and in the shadow of death, to guide our feet into the way of peace. And the child grew, and waxed strong in spirit, and was in the deserts till the day of his shewing unto Israel." Luke 1:78-80

"The light of the body is the eye: therefore when thine eye is single, thy whole body also is full of light; but when thine eye is evil, thy body also is full of darkness." Luke 11:34

God is calling us to a full separation from the world, but we have been so entwined with the world that the Holy Spirit is grieving for His inheritance. The church is trying to please men's souls, to keep them in their seats, trading the anointing for entertainment, trading the Gospel for philosophy, traditions, and science, trading in the power of God for explanations, compromise, and religion. We must allow the glory in and the smoke machine out. The Devil is a

4

counterfeiter and a deceiver. He works through witchcraft that gets its power from the flesh. This brings enmity between man and God. We ask why God is not showing up in the majority of fellowships. This is the answer: God is spirit and those that worship Him must worship Him in Spirit and in Truth.

"But the hour cometh, and now is, when the true worshippers shall worship the Father in spirit and in truth: for the Father seeketh such to worship him."

John 4:23

"Be ye not unequally yoked together with unbelievers: for what fellowship hath righteousness with unrighteousness? And what communion hath light with darkness? And what concord hath Christ with Belial? Or what part hath he that believeth with an infidel? And what agreement hath the temple of God with idols? For ye are the temple of the living God; as God hath said, I will dwell in them, and walk in them; and I will be their God, and they shall be my people. Wherefore come out from among them, and be ye separate, saith the Lord, and touch not the unclean thing; and I will receive you. And will be a Father unto you, and ye shall be my sons and daughters, saith the Lord Almighty." 2 Corinthians 6:14-18

God came into the world not to condemn but to save. Salt and light change the atmosphere.

The only way to do this is by bowing to the Holy Spirit. Do you realize that worship is not a song? It's a lifestyle. There is no such thing as worship music. It is something we use to help us worship God, but it is just music. God does not want music to worship Him. He wants you, and it does not come from lifting hands. It comes from a prostate lifestyle, a humble and rejoicing and obedient heart, a heart that is fully His.

To truly worship God we must truly believe that He is on the throne, that He is glorious, and we must follow His Word with fear and trembling.

He will pour out His grace and anointing to allow us to be able to do that. That's what He does. Then your life is a worship song to Him as the fire of God burns out all the impure things that have come in from the world. Then the opened gates, *His* gates, will swing wide open and the Lord of Glory will come in. Until Jesus is fully on the throne of our hearts, it is impossible to worship Him in Spirit and in Truth. He wants total surrender. Then you will be the light of the World. Then you can go into darkness and shine, shine, shine. Miracles, signs and wonders will be normal to you, and the natural will be abnormal to you.

"That they all might be damned who believed not the truth, but had pleasure in unrighteousness. But we are bound to give thanks always to God for you, brethren beloved of the Lord, because God hath from the beginning chosen you to salvation through sanctification of the Spirit and belief of the truth:

Whereunto he called you by our gospel, to the obtaining of the glory of our Lord Jesus Christ." 2 Thessalonians 2:12-14

"Who by him do believe in God, that raised him up from the dead, and gave him glory; that your faith and hope might be in God." 1 Peter 1:21

When we live in the flesh, it is impossible to walk in the Spirit, and His spirit is light. So God wants to till the garden of our hearts and also to clean up all demonic traffic in our sanctuaries: our houses and our hearts. Remember Eli? We must come out of Babylon. We must expose this harlot for who she is and all her false prophets. All her flesh teaching, all heresies, must come under the light. God will have His bride. He will! It is best that we let Him work and work with Him to pluck out these corruptible seeds. God is not mocked. What you sow you will reap.

"Be not deceived; God is not mocked: for whatsoever a man soweth, that shall he also reap. For he that soweth to his flesh shall of the flesh reap corruption; but he that soweth to the Spirit shall of the Spirit reap life everlasting. And let us not be weary in well doing: for in due season we shall reap, if we faint not." Galatians 6:7-9

So this is a book of blessing. Carnal preachers or soothsayers make God a sugar daddy, saying that He will cancel debt but leave you in a mess. He will cancel debt after you repent and He fixes the foundation (the reason

7

you got into debt in the first place), but that is where carnal ministers stop. There is always a, "IF you do this...", and God always follows with, "I will do this...."

Action and reaction. We must guard the purity of truth and dispose of the work of the Nicolatians. This book will open your eyes to see the Truth! We are not here to build a golden calf. We are here to build the wall. God is building a house, but He must first show us the house. Everything that is not built on the rock, the sure foundation, will fall while false prophets are saying, "Peace, peace..." God is saying, "Turn from your wicked ways. Repent! Clean your houses." God is saying, "I will throw those that allow the teaching of Jezebel into a sick bed with her." Do you think He was just having a bad day? All the grace preachers are only giving you part of the message. You will see. This book has been written by the Holy Spirit - that means those that have an ear to hear will hear what the Spirit is saying to the church. God is restoring the ancient paths. He is provoking jealousy to His chosen, Israel. He needs a new man, but until righteousness prevails, He will not allow harlotry and purity to live together. It's time for Sampson to grow his hair back. Get your joy! Walk in your anointing. Put Delilah away for good. What if the wealth of the wicked was greed in the body of Christ? What if your god was greed? Mammon is another god in the Body of Christ that needs to be smashed. The house of Dagon is coming down.

"And the Philistines took the ark of God, and brought it from Ebenezer unto Ashdod. When the Philistines took the ark of God, they brought it into the house of Dagon, and set it by Dagon. And when they of Ashdod arose early on the morrow, behold, Dagon was fallen upon his face to the earth before the ark of the LORD. And they took Dagon, and set him in his place again." 1 Samuel 5:2-3

The scriptures will manifest the Truth. The Truth will set us free! See? We cannot serve God and gods, but some will tell you or deceive you that God wants you to gain the whole world because you are the head and not the tail, but Jesus clearly said, "Give up this life to receive life." Then He said He has come to give you the abundant life. So how can we give up this life to receive life? Fullness of life comes from dying to the world. This kingdom will spring forth, and you will have all that you need: cars, houses, land and 100 times more, but when and only when you give up this life! God is on the throne, leading the way and making every crooked way straight.

"But seek ye first the kingdom of God, and his righteousness; and all these things shall be added unto you." Matthew 6:33

9

We have charlatans on television telling people to be in fear, telling them to store up! False! Jesus said not to worry about tomorrow. We must learn to follow Christ. He will multiply what we give Him. We must come out of Babylon.

We must put our trust in Him – a supernatural God - and in His kingdom that cannot be shaken. Jesus rebuked us about storing up our treasure to heap in the last days. Then He tells us that our vats will overflow. Is He confused? No. Some of us have been hearing half truth. All these promises are for those walking in faith, in the Spirit of Truth and love. The others are those that continue to depend on their own strength, their own wisdom and their own folly. God wants His church to be Spirit led, not program led, not carnal, because He is spiritual. We are about to embark on a trip to the Promised Land, but only the remnant will be in full access. Choose this day who you will serve!

"For let not that man think that he shall receive any thing of the Lord. A double minded man is unstable in all his ways."
James 1:7-8

Elijah was drawing a line. If Baal be your god, serve Him, but if God be your God, serve Him. Let us expose all the things that contaminate His houses of worship. He has told us to let Him in. He stands at the door. He will not compete with other gods.

In this book, God will put eye solvent on your eyes so that you may see! He wants us hot. He wants us hungry and poor in spirit. He promises to fill us with every good thing that comes from above. Are you ready? *Smashing Deception in the House of God* is a gate that will conduct your spirit to the Truth, the truth of what God sees, what He hates, and His intense mercy and redemption that is available for us all to repent and to return to the master plan that He has for us here on Earth, as the pure, spotless, shameless bride of Christ!

* The Bible tells us that in "the last days" the pervading influence of a mysterious system known as Babylon will profoundly affect the entire world. **"For all nations have drunk of the wine of the wrath of her fornication, and the kings of the earth have committed fornication with her." Revelation 18:3.** Today, we see not just the nations of the Earth but God's people being made spiritually drunk by this entity called Babylon.

MY WHEEL INSIDE THE WHEEL
The five-fold ministries

"I want my wheel moving in my church. I am the wheel inside the wheel. The five spokes that hold the wheel in place are my five-fold ministries that I have chosen. When you decide to keep a spoke out, there is no balance. There is no unity. I have set in place apostles, prophets, evangelists, pastors and teachers. These are offices set in place by Me in the local body as well as in regions. This is the reformation: the bones coming alive. The muscles on the bone are power and unity - this is what holds the structure together. When I am moving in the church, give full submission to My Spirit. When you decide you don't need one part, my body is deformed. Cut off an ear and even a toe, I limp. I use different people in different ways. I have established seers in My House for the good of the Body, those who see what I show them, not what man says, not advisers of men placed by men, but overseers, not from a distance but within. I have set offices in My House, over regions and in the local church. All of you can move in gifts, but I have offices that I have set in place. As you fill those offices, my framework is in place. This last day move will

happen when everything is removed that has been placed by men."

The above word came from this dream: I was standing in the House of God. There were bright orange tiles. The entire room was set with these tiles. There was one small area in the middle that was set in elbow macaroni. The floor was the focus.

My natural father was representing God. He said, "Show them." Over to the left of me was a bag of cement. I picked up one of the tiles and started scraping the elbow macaroni off. I looked at the bag of cement and said, "Can we use that?" The dream ended and then the Holy Spirit revealed what the dream meant.

Here is the interpretation of the dream: The mortar represents what God has sitting, waiting to be used. Macaroni are man-made perishable things. The movement of the elbow means to remove or to shove out of the way. These things in the foundation of the church that are man-made are not eternal. That is an area in the church that God wants to remove.

When this act of obedience is done, God is going to show up like He has never shown up before. As long as these hindrances are in place, in this section or area, they need to be removed and replaced with what God has ordained and anointed to be there: the five-fold ministries.

ALIGNMENT IN THE BODY

"Church, line up." God says,
"Now is time for an apostolic alignment."

God has various anointing gifts working in one place, coming together for edification, exhortation and correction – one teaching the other. Do all prophecy? Do all teach? Do all??? There are people God has anointed and has/is bringing into specific places. Gifts are just sitting and being wasted. They are there to build up the Body. There are people who need what others have. People are coming to different places where they can't stay because they are not getting what they need when they come together. This is a sign that nobody has recognized the Body and its members.

"For he that eateth and drinketh unworthily, eateth and drinketh damnation to himself, not discerning the Lord's body." 1 Corinthians 11:29

Gifts have to go to places because they are bringing something that is needed. "Church, line up." God says, "Now is the time that we need apostolic alignment." God has given all different gifts, mantles, and anointing for the work of the ministry and the equipping of the saints. When leaders hide the gifts in the back room, they are saying, "Hey, Jesus, we don't want you to operate here. Just sit down and listen."

When we don't allow full operation of the Spirit, this is exactly how God sees it. Man's order must be shut down and full alliance must take place for regions to be shaken. Something else the Lord showed me is this: apostle, prophet, evangelist, pastor and teacher – is the fivefold ministry. The New Testament spoke about "pastor" only one time. Other ministry gifts are spoken about more than others. Why is this? We always think the pastor is the leader of the church. Why are we so programmed, including me? I was guilty of this myself saying, "Pastor," so freely.

Ephesians 4:1 is the one place it is mentioned. Paul is clearly saying in **Ephesians 4:2-7,** with lowliness and meekness, longsuffering, forbearing one another in love: one body and one Spirit - one faith and one God. One is given the grace according to the gift. So everybody is trying to be a pastor. We have created this to be a high calling. None of these gifts are better or higher than the other. They reveal Jesus altogether--without this we look like a one-headed freak. Our high calling is to be like Him!

The Bible reads in **Ephesians 4:16: "From whom the whole body fitly joined together compacted by that which every joint supplies according to be effectual working in the measure of every part, making increase of the body to every part, unto the edifying of itself."**

So we all need to move in God. Not one preferred over the other. A high calling should be whatever God has called you to do. Come on, Church, when the enemy gets a pastor with a lukewarm message, a compromising message, a message that always tickles your ears with such a positive message, the enemy is able to deceive and destroy not just the leader but the whole Body. This is because Jesus was not allowed to bring all of Himself in, and Jezebel is now polluting the Body. Now let's go to **1 Corinthians 12:28: "God has set some in the church; first apostles, second prophets, thirdly teacher, after that miracles, then gifts of healings, helps, governments, diversity of tongues."** God gave Paul these revelations. Now God is giving them to us.

Back up to this passage:

"For our comely parts have no need; but God has tempered the Body together, having given more abundant honor to the part which lacked so there should be no schisms in the Body, that the members should have the same care for one another."
1 Corinthians 12:24

We certainly have enough pastors in the Body of Christ and all these titles are not even in the Bible: Youth Pastor, Music Pastor, and Pastor for everything. Too many pastors, but not enough helps. So let's honor the helps. Let's carry their bags. Wouldn't it be funny if we walked around saying, "Hello, Helps?" "Good morning, Gifts of Healing." "Gifts of Healing, have you seen Miracles, today?" "Go ask Pastor, or maybe Apostle, if they have seen him," or do you mean Miracle Johnny or Miracle Teddy? Wouldn't that be

16

dumb? That's what we are doing: man worship. And the enemy started it all.

That's why Jesus washed his disciples' feet. He was a prophet. He was a pastor. He was an evangelist and so on. He said that they wouldn't understand, but there will come a time when they will understand. Now is that time. Come on, Church. We need to trade our titles for some revelation and some compassion. We need to follow the entire scriptures not just one we take out of context and make our own. God told me that when the churches yield to the gifts, it is the same as yielding to Christ Himself, and they will have all the glory, power, and anointing that has never been seen before, the latter and the former rain. Don't think that you really have something if you are operating in your religious man-made structure. It will surely pass away.

We, as a church, are told in **1 Corinthians 12:31** to earnestly covet the best gifts, but do not covet the carrier of the gift. We love every pastor. We need you all so much and all that you do for the body of Christ. We honor you for that and for all your time. However, this is a call from the throne of God to set order in the house of God--not to pick on anyone--but to open the eyes of the blind, the religious. If you are offended at this word then maybe you need to hit your knees and ask Him why! Love is not puffed up!

DIFFERENCES THAT DEFINE
THE TRUE CHURCH OF CHRIST & ITS TRUE LEADERS

"See, I have this day appointed you to the oversight of the nations and of the kingdoms to root out and pull down, to destroy and to overthrow, to build and to plant." Jeremiah 1:10 (AMP King James Version)

This is what you are about to see: "What God is doing and what the Church will look like and won't look like, says the Lord!" The rise of the apostolic church, God spoke to me seven years ago and said, "I am doing a new thing, but it is really an old thing: restoring my governmental church. I will plant one forerunner in a cave in every region. Raise him up."

{ THE FOUR STAGES }

1) Planting: Sets a forerunner apostle in a region and territory.
2) Warfare and training of apostles and prophets of the house, taking spiritual ground.

3) Building the house: Jesus as cornerstone on the foundation of the apostolic and prophetic. Helps and miracles and God's government set in order.

4) Hub, the house, the filling station, the revival port, the apostolic center; positioned where teams go in and out throughout the nation and nations of the World; gathering apostles, prophets, evangelists, pastors, teachers, coming in and going out! ECCLESIASTIC!

{ WHAT IT WILL LOOK LIKE }

1) It will cast out demons.

2) It will preach sound doctrine.

3) It will expose satanic activity.

4) It will expose false teaching.

5) It will equip the saints.

6) It will impart gifts of the Holy Ghost.

7) It will spiritually discern a matter with God's eyes not outward with the eyes of man.

8) It will be God pleasing not man pleasing. It will not tolerate rebellion and witchcraft.

9) It will demonstrate God's love, not talk about it.

10) It will be a place of miracles, signs, and wonders. Souls will be transformed. The real church arising and the gates of hell will and cannot prevail.

11) It will prepare people to be witnesses (martyrs) for Christ. Living to die - dying to live.

12) It will have people in love with Jesus and one another, not attacking its own body but building itself up in love, truth, and grace.

{ WHAT IT WILL NOT LOOK LIKE }

1) It will not be pastoral: There is no such thing as a worship pastor, a youth pastor, a women's pastor, young adult's pastor, and so on. All man-made structure. But it will be governmental without man made membership and control.

2) It will not have board members voting on what to do from flesh, but prophets and five-fold ministers agreeing on the spirit led direction.

3) It will not have programs and programs and more programs and 5013C worldly governmental support, agreements, and mixture.

4) It will not have counselors. The word of God will counsel and the wisdom of God through the gifts of the Holy Spirit.

5) It will not compromise with pagan traditions and pagan rituals and pagan feasts. It will not eat from the tables of devils and the table of the Lord.

6) It will not have man's wisdom, leavened bread: Man's ways, man-made worship, man-made philosophy, and man - made doctrines with no power.

7) It will not have entertainers but true worshipers worshiping in the spirit and in Truth.

8) It will not have children and kid's church. This is another unbiblical tradition. Children will sit right under the anointing and the word and will be spiritually equipped.

20

Jesus said that He is the bread of life and suffer not the little children to come to Him. Train a child in the way he should go and he will not depart from it. Not from children's books but from the word!

9) It will not be a social club.

10) It will not have hierarchy and man worship. On the contrary, the head will wash the feet. The older will serve the younger. The greatest will be the servant of all.

11) It will not charge for conferences. It will not market the Gospel but freely will give what it has freely received.

12) It will not put up with Jezebel or the spirit of Balaam or the spirit of Nicolaitans.

The storm that is coming will expose the old thing because the waves will wash all the sand away. The new thing will be the only thing moving in power and alive! The outpouring will pour the latter and former rain, a double portion of both apostasy and glory. Separation will be so notable. The real church will not be in word only but in power. Look out. Here comes the bride.

14 DIFFERENCES BETWEEN ORGANIZED RELIGION & GOD'S GOVERNMENTAL CHURCH

1) Organized Religion: It is run by board members and puppet pastors placed by man. Governmental Church: Apostles & Prophets and the 5 fold ministries ordained from heaven.

2) Organized Religion: Success means how many people they can get into the building every week to do religious duties. Governmental Church: Success means how many they get sent out in the Spirit and in the Power.

3) Organized Religion: Full of programs, forms, man-made structures. Governmental Church: Casting out demons, healing the sick, raising the dead. They give freely what they freely receive.

4) Organized Religion: They are under rule of carnal government and statues and rules. Governmental Church: They are under God's law, no matter what consequences bring.

5) Organized Religion: It runs like a business with staff and workers' hierarchy. Governmental Church: It runs like a Body functioning as Christ being the head, and His word is final and absolute.

6) Organized Religion: Counseling with worldly sources, psychiatry, mental and physical health, pharoahs' structures. Governmental Church: Counseling with the wisdom from the Spirit and by the Spirit. Inner healing begins in the spirit, through casting out demons and working out salvation. By the power of the Spirit, Sozo happens: Total restoration and redemption in the soul, in the spirit, and in the body.

7) Organized Religion: It fills people with man's wisdom mixed with the care of this life. Governmental Church: It fills people with the Holy Ghost.

8) Organized Religion: They vote on all moves. Governmental Church: They are in one spirit; they move in the Spirit.

9) Organized Religion: They build the house on mortar, clay (Golden calf). Governmental Church: They build temples of God, not made by the hands of man.

10) Organized Religion: They make you a member of their denomination or church sect. Governmental Church: They make disciples.

11) Organized Religion: They tolerate pagan and worldly traditions, and the gates of hell are left open. Governmental Church: They hate the world and the things of it. The gates of hell are closed.

12) Organized Religion: They preach in stories of the Bible, mixing science with philosophies. Governmental Church: They preach sound doctrine, not enticing words of man's wisdom but the Gospel with demonstration of it in power.

13) Organized Religion: They do skits, plays and soulish entertainment that moves the soul. Governmental Church: They seek to feel and to touch everything that is of and from the Spirit. They worship in Spirit and Truth.

14) Organized Religion: It justifies itself in how much and what they do for the cause of their institutions. Governmental Church: It justifies itself by faith and by who they are in Christ!

12 DIFFERENCES BETWEEN
A HIRELING AND A SHEPHERD

1) Hirelings use their position to build their own kingdom. Shepherds use their position to build up the sheep.

2) Hirelings feed and let the sheep eat and drink anything and anywhere. Shepherds lead them by the still waters, making sure they pass by doctrines of demons. (Water is the Word.) Still water meaning lifeless, dead, not living water but man's wisdom, leaven doctrine, but it will direct them to living waters (river, the Spirit).

3) Hirelings instruct and demand. Shepherds raise up sheep like a father.

4) Hirelings smell like money. Shepherds smell like sheep.

5) Hirelings flee when the wolf comes (Satan). It is too much trouble. They don't have time. They protect themselves. Shepherds, when the wolf comes, stand with them and protect their sheep. They fight with and for them, even ripping them out of the wolf's mouth.

6) Hirelings only care about what people think of them, showmen, men-pleasing spirit (Spirit of Saul). Shepherds don't care what people think. They are not man pleasers but God pleasers (Spirit of David).

7) Hirelings run a ministry and a church like a business. The hireling (pastor/leader) is the C.E.O. Shepherds treat and see the sheep as a family. The pastor or apostle fathers the sheep.

8) Hirelings demand to be served. They present guilt to help build their golden calf or their kingdom and call it God's kingdom. Shepherds serve the sheep and lay down their lives for them.

9) Hirelings do not care for their sheep so when the sheep take off or disappear they count the loss. They find ways to attract more, to make merchandise of, and to make slaves. Shepherds leave the 99 to go after the one, even the wayward, to the point of breaking its legs and carrying the sheep for miles.

10) Hirelings do not allow you to connect with them one on one, but you need to make an appointment through the middle man, the secretary of the C.E.O., and then you have 30 minutes. Shepherds make themselves available in time of need then they will filter the situation for need, severity, and importance. They will actually give you their cell phone number, if they are truly a sheep.

11) Hirelings put their own family, their own agenda, before the sheep. Actually they have special grace for them that would never apply to others. In other words, they are

respecters of people. Shepherds treat all with respect and honor, fearing God and maintaining a good report to all.

12) Hirelings withhold correction and reproof and rebuke unless that interferes with their protocol because sheep are just a number and because of the pride they carry within. They want to be the biggest pasture around. Shepherds will get in your stuff and combat the sin you may be in because to them you are a son or a daughter of the Most High. Your eternal soul is what is most important to them.

Watch out for hirelings! Run from them! There are true shepherds, and they will find you and carry you back home.

Jesus Christ is the great shepherd and our example as a leader, laying down His life, preaching truth in the most religious time, standing firm, being hated by the religious organization of His time because He would not allow them to control or manipulate Him!! This is why He gave gifts unto men and said, "Peter, feed my sheep," and do and say what I did and what I am saying. Give them sound doctrine!

"Do **YOU** love Me?" Says the Lord.

"And I will give you pastors according to mine heart, which shall feed you with knowledge and understanding." Jeremiah 3:15

THE CORNERSTONE WHICH THE BUILDERS REJECTED

Part I

"This (JESUS) is the Stone which was despised and rejected by you, the builders, but which has become the Head of the corner (the cornerstone)." Acts 4:11

This cornerstone that the Bible talks about in **Acts 4:11** is Jesus, and He is the foundation according to **Ephesians 2:20**. The religious leaders, Pharisees and Sadducees, were supposed to have lived by the Law of Moses when our Savior had finally come. They were deciding who and when, showing partiality, for example, the woman caught in adultery would not even have been punished. She had been doing this for awhile, but they tried to trap the Lord with their legalistic ways. They were partial. They were willing to kill her to prove that the Master was wrong. There was evil in their hearts. This spirit is still in operation, coming against truth, grace, and the power of God. Today, leaders and pastors are still trying to shut down fresh fire, fresh faith, using their doctrines and opinions. They are still rejecting the cornerstone. They are legalistic. Jesus said that they killed the prophets that came before

Him. Knowing this well, they would also choose to kill him in the name of God. It was blasphemy. Jesus was rebuking man's order in the book of Revelation through the letters to the seven churches. Fear God, Saints! Paul was clearly laying down a foundation. Paul never said, "In this particular place, you are to do something different if you are called to be a gathering of saints subject one to another." Well, you say, "That's not what we do here." So, this is sin. Jesus, Paul, Peter, James, John, and all the rest were moved by the inspiration of the Holy Ghost. Guess what? The Holy Ghost is alive and is still giving inspiration by His own spirit. He will always confirm His word, but you say, "God has us doing something different." No, my friend, you are deciding to create your own Gospel. This is what religion has done, how the devil has gotten in. Now you, with your new title of non-denomination, have created another denomination. It is the same thing. God is done with man's order. He is done with leaders who are more afraid of the people than of Him. This is witchcraft disguised as the Gospel. Rebellion against His Word is sin. Church, you are sinning. You don't even fear who is deceiving you. God is not mocked. He is the same yesterday, today, and forever. He is the same God of love. He will be the same God that sends people to eternal torture because of their own choices. Open your eyes and see. Hear what the Spirit is saying. Do not use the grace of God in vain. Do not be unequally yoked with unbelievers. You continue to lead and run your gathering the way you want to do it, not how God wants it done. Then you say God is doing something different here. He does nothing different apart from His word. It is one body, one mediator, one accord. What do you think? Jesus, the head of the church (**Ephesians 5:23**), is going to tell His people to do a different Gospel than the one down the street? Jesus clearly commanded us to do what He did, not what the Pharisees were doing. What they were doing was not what we should do. We need to do what God is doing. What is your big or small church doing? We need God's power, not enticing words of man. He commanded us by saying: **"Go your way, and tell John what things you have seen and heard; how that the blind see, the lame walk, the lepers are cleansed, the deaf hear, the dead are raised, to the poor the gospel is preached,"** Luke 7:22. Also He said: **"Blessed is He who shall not be offended in me,"** in **Luke 7:23**. Why are we so offended by Jesus? Religious leaders are grieving the Holy Ghost, which is the third part of the trinity. The Father, the Son, Jesus, and the Holy Ghost are one. So you are offended at your Lord. Open up your eyes. Receive the things of the Spirit. Jesus moved in the miraculous every time. There were unsaved seekers as well as the ones who began to follow Him already. Christ in us, the hope of glory (**Colossians 1:27**). God tries to bring His Kingdom to His church, and we are worried about offending the religious, the rebellious. The fear of man is sin. Fear God, not man. Obedience is better than sacrifice (**1 Samuel 15:22**). **"You sacrifice your life and don't obey my Word."** Your sacrifice is not received just like Cain's offering (**Matthew 10:5-8**). This is not a suggestion, Church. Wake up, you are deceived and deceiving others.

30

The last word of Jesus in the book of **Mark, chapter 16, verses 15-20** was: **"And he said unto them, Go ye into all the world, and preach the gospel to every creature. He that believeth and is baptized shall be saved; but he that believeth not shall be damned. And these signs shall follow them that believe; In my name shall they cast out devils; they shall speak with new tongues; They shall take up serpents; and if they drink any deadly thing, it shall not hurt them; they shall lay hands on the sick, and they shall recover."** What is the problem? Man's ways and control. You believe you are the leader of the church. You are full of false humility which is pride.

You are creating heresies. You are holding back the truth and doing it in the name of love. Real love is laying down your life and your will for your brother (**1 John 3:16**). What that really means is becoming a persecuted target for your Lord. You are so fearful of men, of what they think or say, or that you might not get their money that you shimmy through the Gospel, watching your words, killing the anointing. We have a controversial Gospel. You are called to bring controversy against evil like a sword, but you pull out your butter knife and just rub it over their flesh. Jesus said this is a wicked servant. You are not preaching God's truth or demonstrating the kingdom. The kingdom is not in Word only, but in demonstration of power. You seek your board members of flesh instead of God himself. You have gone the way of Cain. Your sacrifices cannot be accepted, but you think everything is okay. You pervert my ways to keep the agendas of man. Look to the book of Revelation where

Jesus speaks to the seven churches. Jesus is speaking to His church for the last day, to over 70% of His church, and Jesus is rebuking them. We have taken His grace and perverted it with heresies and doctrines of devils, soothsaying messages, while people are going to hell. We need truth and the sword and the power of God. Why, Church? Have you really heard people preach on Jesus, rebuking? Witchcraft is operating now. Because these preachers aren't going to preach against themselves, and the seducing spirits have them blind to the truth - not putting the first thing first. This is a crucial time. We must go to the lost sheep and pull our brothers and sisters out of the ditch. If the blind lead the blind, won't they both fall into a ditch? We must shine the light into the darkness into the ditch that has so easily taken the church captive. The truth will set us free. Change your bylaws to God's laws and change your opinions to the Word of God. Look to Jesus, the author and finisher of your faith (**Hebrews 12:2**). His word is truth (**John 17:17**). If you reject the truth, you reject Jesus because He is The Truth (**John 14:6**). Think of that: What kind of thing built by man can stand up without the chief cornerstone?

"For thus it stands in Scripture: Behold, I am laying in Zion a chosen (honored), precious chief Cornerstone, and he who believes in Him (who adheres to, trusts in, and relies on Him) shall never be confound, disappointed or put to shame."

1 Peter 2:6 (Amplified Bible Version)

Brothers, let us no longer reject Him.

THE CORNERSTONE WHICH THE BUILDER REJECTED

Part II

"This (JESUS) is the Stone which was despised and rejected by you, the builders, but which has become the Head of the corner (the cornerstone)." Acts 4:11

We need to put our agendas aside and listen to anointed, holy men and women of God who move in the Spirit. We need the Holy Spirit moving, doing, working among us. Clear your mind and now think on this: Father, Son, and Holy Ghost – they are one. The Holy Spirit is God: His best gift to us, His first, was His son. He gave everything so we could have his spirit, to duplicate Him. When we reject the things of the Spirit, we reject God.

"I am the vine, you are the branches. He who abides in Me, and I in him, bears much fruit; for without Me you can do nothing." John 15:5

This is pride. Hiding behind false humility, we say one thing and do another. We all want to take cities, nations. "You think you can do it without the manifestation of my

Spirit," says God. That's pride. Works are dead without the Holy Spirit. It is like being in a canoe trying to paddle against the wind, upstream. The Kingdom is God's business. We look at others trying to see how their churches grow. A church explodes, and they write a book on what and how they did it, such as, "*Five Ways to Multiply Your Church.*" What's next? "Every hundredth new person at church for the first time wins a flat screen T.V." Sounds ridiculous, but really that's what is going on.

What happened to **Mark 16**, the great commission: Casting out devils, speaking in new tongues, healing the sick, baptizing in the Holy Ghost and fire?

I think God knows best how to build His own church. We need to lay down fear of man. Fear God. Do not allow heresies and seducing spirits in. Seeker friendly deception - this is also pride. You think you have a better way to reach people. Peter reached and converted 3000 in a day. How? With the Holy Ghost! God is not looking for a church full of seekers of friendly messages. Repent! The kingdom of God is at hand. Church attending is not what God wants. He wants disciples. What are disciples? They are supposed to be followers of Christ doing greater things than the master did.

"Most assuredly, I say to you, he who believes in Me, the works that I do he will do also; and greater works than these he will do, because I go to My Father." John 14:12.

Disciples of Jesus Christ do not leave things up to some hot shot preacher who continually talks about the things of God but never operates in them. They are always doing exploits.

"For the kingdom of God is not in word but in power."
1 Corinthians 4:20

They are always learning but never coming to the knowledge of the truth, just like it is written in **2 Timothy 3:7, "Always learning and never able to come to the knowledge of the truth."**

The people are crying out for truth. Here it is: His kingdom will come just as it is in heaven no matter what man wants or tradition tries to keep. This is the day of the Lord. This is time to take back the kingdom. It is time for the latter rain to fall. Look out, America. Here comes the real Church.

"But know this, that in the last days perilous times will come: For men will be lovers of themselves, lovers of money, boasters, proud, blasphemers, disobedient to parents, unthankful, unholy, unloving, unforgiving, slanderers, without self-control, brutal, despisers of good, traitors, headstrong, haughty, lovers of pleasure rather than lovers of God, having a form of godliness but denying its power. And from such people turn away! For of this sort are those who creep into households and make captives of gullible women loaded down with sins, led away by various lusts, always learning and never able to come to the knowledge of the truth." 2 Timothy 3:1-7

This is happening now, especially in the church. It goes on in this chapter and gets worse and worse. Choose what team you are on. Make audible repentance first. Be filled with the Holy Ghost.

"Preach the word; be instant in season, out of season; reprove, rebuke, exhort with all long suffering and doctrine. For the time will come when they will not endure sound doctrine; but after their own lusts shall they heap to themselves teachers, having itching ears; And they shall turn away their ears from the truth, and shall be turned unto fables. But watch thou in all things, endure afflictions, do the work of an evangelist, make full proof of thy ministry." 2 Timothy 4:2-5

A big lie from the enemy is this: "Well, we have all kinds of people here. We need to be careful. We don't want to scare them away." When did Jesus change his gospel? Everyone to whom He preached was not even born again, not even birthed yet, until He manifested the kingdom. The church has a lot of people who are not saved. They won't be saved if you think you can save them your way. The fullness of the gospel is the only way to save a soul, by the power of God. This is the greatest miracle!

Love will draw them. How can they believe if they do not see Jesus revealed and His power manifested? Great worship does not save us. Great speakers cannot save us. Big churches cannot save us. Imagine Jesus Christ walking 3 1/2 years with no power, just talking about himself, but never showing any proof of His power. He just had meetings and preached and talked about himself. NO demonstration at all.

That's what many are doing: talking about Jesus, not being Jesus. Do you think His church would exist if Jesus held back His power and only used enticing words? We can be like Jesus now. That's our calling. You say, "We don't want to scare them away." Believe you will scare them to Jesus. Supernaturally! His power proves He is. Every religion is full of words. God commands through Paul to reject churches or gathering places that deny the power of God. **"Having a form of godliness but denying its power." (2 Timothy 3:5)** Let's turn away from such people!

Becoming a disciple is not serving at church, a denomination, or a religion. It is becoming and doing the works that Jesus did. **"Most assuredly, I say to you, he who believes in Me, the works that I do he will do also; and greater works than these he will do, because I go to My Father." John 14:12**

Don't ever say that we don't want to offend them.

"And blessed is he who is not offended because of Me." Matthew 11:6

Don't ever be ashamed of Him, of His power, or of His Holy Spirit.

"For I am not ashamed of the gospel of Christ, for it is the power of God to salvation for everyone who believes, for the Jew first and also for the Greek." Romans 1:16

Jesus said, "If you deny me, I will deny you, too." Father, Son, and Holy Ghost are one. You cannot deny one and not offend the other. So, my friend, open up the church and bring the real thing. We don't need another play or skit. The church is not supposed to be a talent show. Trade the show for testimonies and demonstration of power. People are saying, "Show me the way." How do we show them without the proof? Holy Spirit is our proof: **"For you will be His witness to all men of what you have seen and heard." Acts 22:15**

The Bible speaks of what you have SEEN and heard!

Those seekers that you are trying not to offend will just go on down the road seeking for the real thing. You will lose them anyway. The reason they are seeking in the first place is for the real thing. We have put Him in a back room in some box. Take Him out. Let God be God and open His ark and release His glory in His house. People are seeking the glory. We have been bewitched by the enemy.

Run into the power of the Holy Ghost. God has His way of reaching His people. The Church belongs to Him.

"And He put all things under His feet, and gave Him to be head over all things to the church." Ephesians 1:22.

Lay down your pride, your way. Put on Christ and see the harvest come running to Him. Many are deceived; many believe the Holy Spirit is moving in His fullness, but He is not. The devil, the deceiver, wants to make many think something different. When He moves, you will know. You will see the fruits - thousands coming to Christ in one day! Leaders, don't settle for the brass, go for the gold. As we, as a body, come together, yielding to God, He will move mountains. Remember, without faith it is impossible to please Him. We can no longer stand in the way of God. He must be the head of everything, not man and his religious hierarchy system. We cannot become like Saul and do things our way. This is witchcraft. Seek his face, fear God, and watch His harvest come rushing in. Our prayer must be, "Not my will but yours, Father." Jesus put His own will down and said, "Not my will but your will be done." Why don't we do the same? Then let's get out of His way. This is how we shake cities, nations, and kingdoms. Together we can do this. Don't say the harvest is in four months. It's here. It's for now. Reapers, reap it.

"Now by this we know that we know Him, if we keep His commandments. He who says, "I know Him," and does not keep His commandments, is a liar, and the truth is not in him. But whoever keeps His word, truly the love of God is perfected in him. By this we know that we are in Him. He who says he abides in Him ought himself also to walk just as He walked."

1 John 2:3-6

BEWARE OF THE LEAVEN
Part I

Many shall come in my name, but beware of them for they are not of me. Can the Spirit of Truth come together with the spirit of error, the works of the flesh? Black & white means the Word of God, darkness and light, good and evil. We are either black or white. What happens when these two come together? It changes identity, neither one nor the other - totally different - Gray! Compromise! The Word of God is very rare in the land. Actually, famine is all over the world. Yes, we have long lectures: How to become a better you; How to get prosperous; How to reach your destiny in life. Now, I am going to motivate you to repent! This Word has been adulterated, Workers of Iniquity! You say, "How can you talk as though you know all?" but he who knows all is the Spirit of Truth. This Spirit is alive and living on the inside. So with all boldness, God is speaking.

Many false prophets and false teachers shall rise in the last days. Paul said that they would be with us. God is raising up the Spirit of Elijah. Yea! Everyone has heard, everyone believes, but when that Spirit is in operation, the same ones deny him (the Spirit of Elijah). That Spirit is the same one that John the Baptist was anointed with. You say, "This can't be God. God is love. He is tender and full or mercy. He would never talk or acts like this." My friend, if you say this in your mind, you are already a candidate to be deceived. You are eating the bread of the Pharisees. You have already started going the wrong way. You have taken the word and made it to no effect. You have been leavened with the leaven of the Pharisees. I am going to preach the WORD and not hold back what God is saying, what God is doing, not what man thinks, not what man wants, not what is politically correct.

Beware of those who:

1) Draw people to themselves.
2) Speak great swelling words of exaggeration.
3) Don't bring the whole counsel of God.
4) Take scripture out of context.
5) Always talk about what God did, not what God is doing.
6) Always say the name of God, but don't mention the name of Jesus Christ.
7) Make their entire sermon a story with no Word in it.
8) Make excuses for God and Jesus Christ.
9) Are so concerned with titles and honoring man.

10) Operate by bringing fear or making you fearful.

Most of all: BEWARE OF THOSE WHO STICK UP for those who do these things and come against those who expose those who are doing these things. Judas and anointing do not mix.

Very rarely will I speak about myself or my encounter, but now the Lord has told me to speak about the little book. I come in the Spirit of Elijah. I come as a messenger of Jesus Christ, not Shane. Let me explain.

"And the angel which I saw stand upon the sea and upon the earth lifted up his hand to heaven, And sware by him that liveth forever and ever, who created heaven, and the things that therein are, and the earth, and the things that therein are, and the sea, and the things which are therein, that there should be time no longer: But in the days of the voice of the seventh angel, when he shall begin to sound, the mystery of God should be finished, as he hath declared to his servants the prophets. And the voice which I heard from heaven spake unto me again, and said, Go and take the little book which is open in the hand of the angel which standeth upon the sea and upon the earth. And I went unto the angel, and said unto him, Give me the little book. And he said unto me, Take it, and eat it up; and it shall make thy belly bitter, but it shall be in thy mouth sweet as honey. And I took the little book out of the angel's hand, and ate it up; and it was in my mouth sweet as

honey: and as soon as I had eaten it, my belly was bitter."
Revelation 10:5-10

Beware of the leaven of the Pharisees. Those who have an ear to hear, hear what the Spirit is saying to the church. Present day truth! Not doctrines of Devils! Here is your motivation:

Step one: Repent!

Step two: Give God all of you.

Step three: Obey him!

Step four: Repent again.

Step five: Obey Him.

Step six: Repent again!

Step seven: Obey Him.

In this is the fullness of joy. Here are your seven steps to victory!

We have made merchandise out of our encounters with God. We have run around prostituting our gift from God. We have made the House of God, the House of Idols, Dagon. We call it our ministry. The Spirit of Judas: this is it! We have allowed relationship without covenant in our midst. The spirit of the world has made merchandise out of His people. Today, we say, "Let God's people go! Beware of the leaven of the Pharisees!"

Many in the Body of Christ want God to call them to itinerant ministry so they can travel, get offerings, and share great revelation or share their gift, but God wants to send His prophets to every church with the spirit of Elijah and take back what is His: The sleeping giant. Many sitting in pews are on their way to hell because the Word of God is not being preached where they are congregating. THE Word, THE LIVING BREAD FROM HEAVEN! Today, God is saying, "Those who have an ear to hear what the Spirit is saying: Listen up!!!!"

Why are we letting soothsayers sooth us out of reality into carnality and deception? If, right now, you are feeling angry at this message, then you may not be at the place with God that you think you are. You may be led by the spirit of error. This is the spirit of truth. This is love and God has shed His blood. Narrow is the way and few are they that find it. Are you one to whom the Lord is going to say, "Well done, good and faithful servant? You told them the truth." Or will you be one to whom He says, "Depart from me, you worker of iniquity?" This saying came out of the mouth of God himself. Interesting: God is not saying this to someone who did not know Him or think he knew Him. This was a worker! Let's get to the scriptures. Show the house to the house!

"I have written unto you, fathers, because ye have known him that is from the beginning. I have written unto you, young

men, because ye are strong, and the word of God abideth in you, and ye have overcome the wicked one. Love not the world, neither the things that are in the world. If any man love the world, the love of the Father is not in him. For all that is in the world, the lust of the flesh, and the lust of the eyes, and the pride of life, is not of the Father, but is of the world. And the world passeth away, and the lust thereof: but he that doeth the will of God abideth for ever. Little children, it is the last time: and as ye have heard that antichrist shall come, even now are there many antichrists; whereby we know that it is the last time. They went out from us, but they were not of us; for if they had been of us, they would no doubt have continued with us: but they went out, that they might be made manifest that they were not all of us. But ye have an unction from the Holy One, and ye know all things. I have not written unto you because ye know not the truth, but because ye know it, and that no lie is of the truth. Who is a liar but he that denieth that Jesus is the Christ? He is antichrist, that denieth the Father and the Son. Whosoever denieth the Son, the same hath not the Father: he that acknowledgeth the Son hath the Father also. Let that therefore abide in you, which ye have heard from the beginning. If that which ye have heard from the beginning shall remain in you, ye also shall continue in the Son, and in the Father. And this is the promise that he hath promised us, even eternal life. These things have I written unto you concerning them that seduce you. But the anointing which ye have received of him abideth in you, and ye need not that any man teach you: but as the same anointing teacheth you of all things, and is truth, and is no lie, and even as it hath taught you, ye shall abide in him. And now, little children, abide in him; that, when he shall appear, we may have confidence, and not be ashamed before him at his coming. If ye know that he is righteous, ye know that every one that doeth righteousness is born of him." 1 John 2:14-29

"And they went into Capernaum; and straightway on the sabbath day he entered into the synagogue, and taught. And they were astonished at his doctrine: for he taught them as one that had authority, and not as the scribes. And there was in their synagogue a man with an unclean spirit; and he cried out, Saying, Let us alone; what have we to do with thee, thou Jesus of Nazareth? Art thou come to destroy us? I know thee who thou art, the Holy One of God. And Jesus rebuked him, saying, Hold thy peace, and come out of him. And when the unclean spirit had torn him, and cried with a loud voice, he came out of him. And they were all amazed, insomuch that they questioned among themselves, saying, What thing is this? What new doctrine is this? For with authority commandeth he even the unclean spirits, and they do obey him." Mark 1:21-27

If you know Him, speak as much as you know about Him, and don't make excuses. Don't give your own opinion. This simple gospel has been made to no effect by religious leaven and by theologians who have the letter without the Spirit, having a form of godliness but denying the power. From such, run away, flee away for your spiritual life, says the Bible. We need to renew our minds, break these mindsets that were set in by the leaven of the Pharisees, like

46

cancer, eating good God cells out of our minds, making the Word of God to no effect!

"For I verily, as absent in body, but present in spirit, have judged already, as though I were present, concerning him that hath so done this deed, In the name of our Lord Jesus Christ, when ye are gathered together, and my spirit, with the power of our Lord Jesus Christ, To deliver such an one unto Satan for the destruction of the flesh, that the spirit may be saved in the day of the Lord Jesus." 1 Corinthians 5:3-5

Handing a Christian over to the enemy is sometimes the best thing to save them. Interesting, right?!

"Your glorying is not good. Know ye not that a little leaven leaveneth the whole lump? 7Purge out therefore the old leaven, that ye may be a new lump, as ye are unleavened. For even Christ our Passover is sacrificed for us: Therefore let us keep the feast, not with old leaven, neither with the leaven of malice and wickedness; but with the unleavened bread of sincerity and truth." 1 Corinthians 5:6-8

Wow! So is Paul God? Is Paul not a man like you and me? So why was he able to discern and judge back then, and now, when somebody else does the same, this person is shut down by the church?

"Ye hypocrites, well did Esaias prophesy of you, saying, This people draweth nigh unto me with their mouth, and honoureth me with their lips; but their heart is far from me." Matthew 15:7-8

This spirit is here again.

"But in vain they do worship me, teaching for doctrines the commandments of men. And he called the multitude, and said unto them, Hear, and understand: Not that which goeth into the mouth defileth a man; but that which cometh out of the mouth, this defileth a man. Then came his disciples, and said unto him, Knowest thou that the Pharisees were offended, after they heard this saying? But he answered and said, Every plant, which my heavenly Father hath not planted, shall be rooted up. Let them alone: they be blind leaders of the blind. And if the blind lead the blind, both shall fall into the ditch."

Matthew 15:9-14

So when you get offended, you are coming against God and His word!

"But those things which proceed out of the mouth come forth from the heart; and they defile the man."

Matthew 15:18

This is the leaven of the Pharisees! This is still sifting. He still has prophet and apostle. How dare we call ourselves prophets just because we get a dream, hear, and then prophecy? God's end time prophets have the spirit of Elijah. Those who have an ear to hear, hear! Prophets will not let God's house turn into a house of idols like Dagon! They will not eat or serve the leaven of the Pharisees!

48

"Then Jesus said unto them, Take heed and beware of the leaven of the Pharisees and of the Sadducees. And they reasoned among themselves, saying, It is because we have taken no bread. Which when Jesus perceived, he said unto them, O ye of little faith, why reason ye among yourselves, because ye have brought no bread? Do ye not yet understand, neither remember the five loaves of the five thousand, and how many baskets ye took up? Neither the seven loaves of the four thousand, and how many baskets ye took up? How is it that ye do not understand that I spake it not to you concerning bread, that ye should beware of the leaven of the Pharisees and of the Sadducees? Then understood they how that he bade them not beware of the leaven of bread, but of the doctrine of the Pharisees and of the Sadducees. When Jesus came into the coasts of Caesarea Philippi, he asked his disciples, saying, Whom do men say that I the Son of man am? And they said, Some say that thou art John the Baptist: some, Elias; and others, Jeremias, or one of the prophets. He saith unto them, But whom say ye that I am?" Matthew 16:6-15

"And the scribes and chief priests heard it, and sought how they might destroy him: for they feared him, because all the people was astonished at his doctrine." Mark 11:18

Also, why would they think Jesus was John or Elisha? That Spirit on Him is the same Spirit! If they asked Jesus that, He must have resembled them in His action and demeanor. We have made Jesus this girly girl. He was bold, and He was strong in Spirit.

"And the blood shall be to you for a token upon the houses where ye are: and when I see the blood, I will pass over you,

49

and the plague shall not be upon you to destroy you, when I smite the land of Egypt. And this day shall be unto you for a memorial; and ye shall keep it a feast to the LORD throughout your generations; ye shall keep it a feast by an ordinance forever. Seven days shall ye eat unleavened bread; even the first day ye shall put away leaven out of your houses: for whosoever eateth leavened bread from the first day until the seventh day, that soul shall be cut off from Israel. And in the first day there shall be an holy convocation, and in the seventh day there shall be an holy convocation to you; no manner of work shall be done in them, save that which every man must eat, that only may be done of you." Exodus 12:13-16

Now you are that temple! YEA! A spiritual house.

"For whoremongers, for them that defile themselves with mankind, for men stealers, for liars, for perjured persons, and if there be any other thing that is contrary to sound doctrine."
1 Timothy 1:10

"As I besought thee to abide still at Ephesus, when I went into Macedonia, that thou mightest charge some that they teach no other doctrine." 1 Timothy 1:3

"That we henceforth be no more children, tossed to and fro, and carried about with every wind of doctrine, by the sleight of men, and cunning craftiness, whereby they lie in wait to deceive." Ephesians 4:14

"Which all are to perish with the using; after the commandments and doctrines of men?" Colossians 2:22

"Take heed unto thyself, and unto the doctrine; continue in them: for in doing this thou shalt both save thyself, and them that hear thee." 1 Timothy 4:16

"Preach the word; be instant in season, out of season; reprove, rebuke, exhort with all long suffering and doctrine."
2 Timothy 4:2

"But speak thou the things which become sound doctrine."
Titus 2:1

Watch out! You cannot eat leavened bread or be partakers or agree with it at all!

"If there come any unto you, and bring not this doctrine, receive him not into your house, neither bid him God speed: For he that biddeth him God speed is partaker of his evil deeds." 2 John 1:10-11

"And they were astonished at his doctrine: for his word was with power." Luke 4:32

Even Jesus could not come up with another doctrine!

"Jesus answered them, and said, My doctrine is not mine, but his that sent me. If any man will do his will, he shall know of the doctrine, whether it be of God, or whether I speak of myself. He that speaketh of himself seeketh his own glory: but he that seeketh his glory that sent him, the same is true, and no unrighteousness is in him." John 7:16-18

51

Jesus is speaking to His church, remember?

"I know thy works, and thy labour, and thy patience, and how thou canst not bear them which are evil: and thou hast tried them which say they are apostles, and are not, and hast found them liars." Revelation 2:2

"But I have a few things against thee, because thou hast there them that hold the doctrine of Balaam, who taught Balac to cast a stumbling block before the children of Israel, to eat things sacrificed unto idols, and to commit fornication. So hast thou also them that hold the doctrine of the Nicolaitanes, which thing I hate." Revelation 2:14-15

What is the biggest idol we have to face: Ourselves! Gospels of self-indulgences and self-promotion. The Word of God is what we need and only what we need. Eat this flesh - The bread of life! The unleavened bread of life! The words I speak, they are spirit, and they are life. Preachers are being led not by the Spirit of God, but by the spirit of Jezebel and the spirit of error! We should not allow that to happen among us because He is not allowing it!

"I know thy works, and charity, and service, and faith, and thy patience, and thy works; and the last to be more than the first. Notwithstanding I have a few things against thee, because thou sufferest that woman Jezebel, which calleth herself a prophetess, to teach and to seduce my servants to commit fornication, and to eat things sacrificed unto idols. And I gave her space to repent of her fornication; and she repented not.

Behold, I will cast her into a bed, and them that commit adultery with her into great tribulation, except they repent of their deeds. And I will kill her children with death; and all the churches shall know that I am he which searcheth the reins and hearts: and I will give unto every one of you according to your works." Revelation 2:19-23

I can boldly say, "If you do not like what I am saying, then you do not like the one who sent me!" He is the one speaking through me!

"But the anointing which ye have received of him abideth in you, and ye need not that any man teach you: but as the same anointing teacheth you of all things, and is truth, and is no lie, and even as it hath taught you, ye shall abide in him."
1 John 2:27

"Beloved, believe not every spirit, but try the spirits whether they are of God: because many false prophets are gone out into the world. ²Hereby know ye the Spirit of God: Every spirit that confesseth that Jesus Christ is come in the flesh is of God: And every spirit that confesseth not that Jesus Christ is come in the flesh is not of God: and this is that spirit of antichrist, whereof ye have heard that it should come; and even now already is it in the world. Ye are of God, little children, and have overcome them: because greater is he that is in you, than he that is in the world. They are of the world: therefore speak they of the world, and the world heareth them. We are of God: he that knoweth God heareth us; he that is not of God heareth not us. Hereby know we the spirit of truth, and the spirit of error." 1 John 4:1-6

"Now the Spirit speaketh expressly, that in the latter times some shall depart from the faith, giving heed to seducing spirits, and doctrines of devils." 1 Timothy 4:1

"Beware of false prophets, which come to you in sheep's clothing, but inwardly they are ravening wolves. Ye shall know them by their fruits. Do men gather grapes of thorns, or figs of thistles? Even so every good tree bringeth forth good fruit; but a corrupt tree bringeth forth evil fruit. A good tree cannot bring forth evil fruit, neither can a corrupt tree bring forth good fruit. Every tree that bringeth not forth good fruit is hewn down, and cast into the fire. Wherefore by their fruits ye shall know them. Not every one that saith unto me, Lord, Lord, shall enter into the kingdom of heaven; but he that doeth the will of my Father which is in heaven. Many will say to me in that day, Lord, Lord, have we not prophesied in thy name? and in thy name have cast out devils? and in thy name done many wonderful works? And then will I profess unto them, I never knew you: depart from me, ye that work iniquity. Therefore whosoever heareth these sayings of mine, and doeth them, I will liken him unto a wise man, which built his house upon a rock: And the rain descended, and the floods came, and the winds blew, and beat upon that house; and it fell not: for it was founded upon a rock. And every one that heareth these sayings of mine, and doeth them not, shall be likened unto a foolish man, which built his house upon the sand: And the rain descended, and the floods came, and the winds blew, and beat upon that house; and it fell: and great was the fall of it. And it came to pass, when Jesus had ended these sayings, the people were astonished at his doctrine: For he taught them as one having authority, and not as the scribes." Matthew 7:15-29

The Holy Spirit inside of you and me!

It's time for the leaders to stop serving leavened bread to the people of God! It's time for the members of the Body to stop eating it! Not only that, it's time to expose the ones who serve what looks like the bread of life, but it's really a puffed up bread, bread without life. If you eat it, you will surely die! Spirit of Truth, come! Open the eyes of God's people! We reject you spirit of error and Jezebel spirit! Come, Holy Spirit! We will not give heed to seducing spirits or wrong teachings. We will not depart from the faith. We will not follow any doctrines of devils because of Him who bought us with great price! Jesus! Come, Spirit of Truth, wisdom and understanding. We love you! We need you now more than ever!

"Buy the truth and do not sell it! Buy wisdom, instruction and understanding." Proverbs 23:23

BEWARE OF THE LEAVEN

Part II

This is now, and in this last message on leaven, we conferred, we investigated, and we have proven that many doctrines of devils are in and around the church and in the so-called assemblies. Is this really the church?

The answer is no! The church is a bride married to a man. That man is Christ Jesus, fully God, fully man. These church organizations and groups are married to the world, running their kingdoms like the world, turning the power of God into no effect, changing themselves into pastors, prophets, and teachers.

They are ministers of Satan, blind leaders who are leading Cains into hell with them because their sacrifice will not be accepted! Some do not even know! They are deceived. They know all about who Jesus was story after story.

They must:

1) Be born again.

2) Repent and turn their back on the world.

3) Believe that He is and that their entire heart is His.

The Lord wants our lives. He laid down His life to give us eternal life in return. He loves us so much. Cain, through the works of His hands, tried to bring God his works. Religion was here in the beginning. Religion is here now, trying to earn our place with God, trying to do things to maintain our Christian title, but relationship is all that the Lord had in mind from the beginning of time until now. The only way to become like Him is to be set apart, holy, just as He is holy. We are in Him. He is in us.

"Adam knew Eve his wife; and she conceived, and bare Cain, and said, I have gotten a man from the LORD. And she again bare his brother Abel. And Abel was a keeper of sheep, but Cain was a tiller of the ground. And in process of time it came to pass, that Cain brought of the fruit of the ground an offering unto the LORD. And Abel, he also brought of the firstlings of his flock and of the fat thereof. And the LORD had respect unto Abel and to his offering: But unto Cain and to his offering he had not respect. And Cain was very wroth, and his countenance fell. And the LORD said unto Cain, Why art thou wroth? and why is thy countenance fallen? If thou doest well, shalt thou not be accepted? and if thou doest not well, sin lieth at the door. And unto thee shall be his desire, and thou shalt rule over him. And Cain talked with Abel his brother: and it came to pass, when they were in the field, that Cain rose up against Abel his brother, and slew him. And the LORD said unto Cain, Where is Abel thy brother? And he said, I know not: Am I my brother's keeper? And he said, What hast thou done? the voice of thy brother's blood crieth unto me from the ground." Genesis 4:1-10

In this process of time, we become that vessel, that living sacrifice, fully acceptable to the Lord. How about surrendering, trusting Him in every area of your life, not just the ones that are a mess or are holding you back? All! Mind, body, soul, spirit! Being a sweet savor to Him! The more you become like Christ, the more you can see the leaven, smell the leaven. It's like God separates you to Himself then separates you more and more until, finally, He is separating you from the so-called Christians. Then He separates you again, opening up your eyes through the true, uncompromised Word, an eye-opening solvent, a washing of the Word. This is why Satan is in many denominations. Man made messes think they know more than God. Reprobates to their faith giving heed to fables!

Wow! Let us look at the fable: Satan – the author of apostasy.

1) We are warned not to take heed to fables.

2) A fable is a story out of the soulish realm to keep you interested.

3) Fables bring the word of God to no effect

4) Fable means fairytale.

What is a tale? It is a lie. Where do lies generate? From a lying spirit. Call them ghost stories. Call them allegories. They are turning the house of prayer into plays, scripts mixing the arts in with the Word, entertaining people instead of correcting, instructing, advising, edifying, warning and preaching.

We do not have to be religious when we are righteous. We do not have to be legalistic to be righteous. We only need Holy Spirit and the Word and a heart open to God.

"Paul, an apostle of Jesus Christ by the commandment of God our Saviour, and Lord Jesus Christ, which is our hope; Unto Timothy, my own son in the faith: Grace, mercy, and peace, from God our Father and Jesus Christ our Lord. As I besought thee to abide still at Ephesus, when I went into Macedonia, that thou mightest charge some that they teach no other doctrine, Neither give heed to fables and endless genealogies, which minister questions, rather than godly edifying which is in faith: so do. Now the end of the commandment is charity out of a pure heart, and of a good conscience, and of faith unfeigned: From which some having swerved have turned aside unto vain jangling; Desiring to be teachers of the law; understanding neither what they say, nor whereof they affirm. But we know that the law is good, if a man use it lawfully; Knowing this, that the law is not made for a righteous

man, but for the lawless and disobedient, for the ungodly and for sinners, for unholy and profane, for murderers of fathers and murderers of mothers, for manslayers, For whoremongers, for them that defile themselves with mankind, for men stealers, for liars, for perjured persons, and if there be any other thing that is contrary to sound doctrine." 1 Timothy 1:1-10

"I charge thee therefore before God, and the Lord Jesus Christ, who shall judge the quick and the dead at his appearing and his kingdom; Preach the word; be instant in season, out of season; reprove, rebuke, exhort with all long suffering and doctrine. For the time will come when they will not endure sound doctrine; but after their own lusts shall they heap to themselves teachers, having itching ears; And they shall turn away their ears from the truth, and shall be turned unto fables. But watch thou in all things, endure afflictions, do the work of an evangelist, make full proof of thy ministry."

2 Timothy 4:1-5

"Now the Spirit speaketh expressly, that in the latter times some shall depart from the faith, giving heed to seducing spirits, and doctrines of devils; Speaking lies in hypocrisy; having their conscience seared with a hot iron; Forbidding to marry, and commanding to abstain from meats, which God hath created to be received with thanksgiving of them which believe and know the truth. For every creature of God is good, and nothing to be refused, if it be received with thanksgiving: For it is sanctified by the word of God and prayer. If thou put the brethren in remembrance of these things, thou shalt be a good minister of Jesus Christ, nourished up in the words of faith and of good doctrine, whereunto thou hast attained. But refuse profane and old wives' fables, and exercise thyself rather unto godliness. For bodily exercise profiteth little: but godliness is profitable unto all things, having promise of the life that now is, and of that which is to come. This is a faithful saying and worthy of all acceptation. ¹⁰For therefore we both labour and suffer reproach, because we trust in the living God, who is the Saviour of all men, specially of those that believe. These things command and teach." 1 Timothy 4:1-11

"For a bishop must be blameless, as the steward of God; not selfwilled, not soon angry, not given to wine, no striker, not given to filthy lucre; But a lover of hospitality, a lover of good men, sober, just, holy, temperate; Holding fast the faithful word as he hath been taught, that he may be able by sound doctrine both to exhort and to convince the gainsayers. For there are many unruly and vain talkers and deceivers, specially they of the circumcision: Whose mouths must be stopped, who subvert whole houses, teaching things which they ought not, for filthy lucre's sake. One of themselves, even a prophet of their own, said, the Cretians are always liars, evil beasts, slow bellies. This witness is true. Wherefore rebuke them sharply, that they may be sound in the faith; ¹⁴Not giving heed to Jewish fables, and commandments of men, that turn from the truth. Unto the pure all things are pure: but unto them that are defiled and unbelieving is nothing pure; but even their mind and conscience is defiled. They profess that they know God; but in works they deny him, being abominable, and disobedient, and unto every good work reprobate."

Titus 1:7-16

"Wherefore the rather, brethren, give diligence to make your calling and election sure: for if ye do these things, ye shall never fall: For so an entrance shall be ministered unto you abundantly into the everlasting kingdom of our Lord and Saviour Jesus Christ. Wherefore I will not be negligent to put you always in remembrance of these things, though ye know them, and be established in the present truth. Yea, I think it meet, as long as I am in this tabernacle, to stir you up by putting you in remembrance; Knowing that shortly I must put off this my tabernacle, even as our Lord Jesus Christ hath shewed me. Moreover I will endeavour that ye may be able after my decease to have these things always in remembrance. For we have not followed cunningly devised fables, when we made known unto you the power and coming of our Lord Jesus Christ, but were eyewitnesses of his majesty. For he received from God the Father honour and glory, when there came such a voice to him from the excellent glory, This is my beloved Son, in whom I am well pleased. And this voice which came from heaven we heard, when we were with him in the holy mount. We have also a more sure word of prophecy; whereunto ye do well that ye take heed, as unto a light that shineth in a dark place, until the day dawn, and the day star arise in your hearts: Knowing this first, that no prophecy of the scripture is of any private interpretation. For the prophecy came not in old time by the will of man: but holy men of God spake as they were moved by the Holy Ghost." 2 Peter 1:10-21

Genealogy means history, tracing lineages, tradition of family and cultures, pursuing bloodlines, family trees, names, and ethnic groups.

There are two trees in the garden: (1) the knowledge of good and evil and (2) the tree of life. Satan fills our heads with pride.

The word says knowledge puffs up. Leaven puffs up! The gospel was given as simple truths that we are called to keep. It is simple and it is power! Theology without the anointing equals = zero. Consuming yourself in the letter equals being tripped up.

The Word of God always divides what is real and what is not, what is God's and what is not. Examples: Cain – Abel / Esau – Jacob / Vessels of honor – Vessels of dishonor / Unrighteous – Righteous / Tares – Wheat / Goats – Sheep / Foolish virgins – Wise virgins

Come on. Shall I go on?

These things are brought into the church by Satan to bring confusion and make the Word of no effect. We must study the teacher, the Rabbi Himself, YESHUA!

"That we henceforth be no more children, tossed to and fro, and carried about with every wind of doctrine, by the sleight of men, and cunning craftiness, whereby they lie in wait to deceive." Ephesians 4:14

"Which all are to perish with the using; after the commandments and doctrines of men?" Colossians 2:22

"And they were astonished at his doctrine: for his word was with power." Luke 4:32

"And I, brethren, when I came to you, came not with excellency of speech or of wisdom, declaring unto you the testimony of

God. For I determined not to know anything among you, save Jesus Christ, and him crucified. And I was with you in weakness, and in fear, and in much trembling. And my speech and my preaching was not with enticing words of man's wisdom, but in demonstration of the Spirit and of power: That your faith should not stand in the wisdom of men, but in the power of God. Howbeit we speak wisdom among them that are perfect: yet not the wisdom of this world, nor of the princes of this world, that come to nought: But we speak the wisdom of God in a mystery, even the hidden wisdom, which God ordained before the world unto our glory: Which none of the princes of this world knew: for had they known it, they would not have crucified the Lord of glory. But as it is written, Eye hath not seen, nor ear heard, neither have entered into the heart of man, the things which God hath prepared for them that love him. But God hath revealed them unto us by his Spirit: for the Spirit searcheth all things, yea, the deep things of God. For what man knoweth the things of a man, save the spirit of man which is in him? even so the things of God knoweth no man, but the Spirit of God. Now we have received, not the spirit of the world, but the spirit which is of God; that we might know the things that are freely given to us of God. Which things also we speak, not in the words which man's wisdom teacheth, but which the Holy Ghost teacheth; comparing spiritual things with spiritual. But the natural man receiveth not the things of the Spirit of God: for they are foolishness unto him: neither can he know them, because they are spiritually discerned. But he that is spiritual judgeth all things, yet he himself is judged of no man. For who hath known the mind of the Lord, that he may instruct him? But we have the mind of Christ." 1 Corinthians 2:1-16

" For ye remember, brethren, our labour and travail: for labouring night and day, because we would not be chargeable unto any of you, we preached unto you the gospel of God. Ye are witnesses, and God also, how holily and justly and unblameably we behaved ourselves among you that believe: As ye know how we exhorted and comforted and charged every one of you, as a father doth his children, That ye would walk worthy of God, who hath called you unto his kingdom and glory." 1 Thessalonians 2:9-12

"Moreover, brethren, I would not that ye should be ignorant, how that all our fathers were under the cloud, and all passed through the sea; And were all baptized unto Moses in the cloud and in the sea; And did all eat the same spiritual meat; And did all drink the same spiritual drink: for they drank of that spiritual Rock that followed them: and that Rock was Christ. But with many of them God was not well pleased: for they were overthrown in the wilderness. Now these things were our examples, to the intent we should not lust after evil things, as they also lusted. Neither be ye idolaters, as were some of them; as it is written, The people sat down to eat and drink, and rose up to play. Neither let us commit fornication, as some of them committed, and fell in one day three and twenty thousand. Neither let us tempt Christ, as some of them also tempted, and were destroyed of serpents. Neither murmur ye, as some of them also murmured, and were destroyed of the destroyer. Now all these things happened unto them for examples: and they are written for our admonition, upon whom the ends of the world are come. Wherefore let him that thinketh he standeth take heed lest he fall. There hath no temptation taken you but such as is common to man: but God is faithful, who will not suffer you to be tempted above that ye are able; but will with the temptation also make a way to escape, that ye may be able to bear it. Wherefore, my dearly beloved, flee from idolatry. I speak as to wise men; judge ye what I say. The cup of blessing which we bless, is it not the communion of the blood of Christ? The bread which we break, is it not the communion of the body of Christ? For we being many are one bread, and one body: for we are all partakers of that one bread. Behold Israel after the flesh: are not they which eat of the sacrifices partakers of the altar? What say I then? That the idol is anything, or that which is offered in sacrifice to idols is anything? But I say, that the things which the Gentiles sacrifice, they sacrifice to devils, and not to God: and I would not that ye should have fellowship with devils. Ye cannot drink the cup of the Lord, and the cup of devils: ye cannot be partakers of the Lord's table, and of the table of devils. Do we provoke the Lord to jealousy? Are we stronger than he? All things are lawful for me, but all things are not expedient: all things are lawful for me, but all things edify not."

1 Corinthians 10:1-23

"As the truth of Christ is in me, no man shall stop me of this boasting in the regions of Achaia. Wherefore? because I love you not? God knoweth. But what I do, that I will do, that I may cut off occasion from them which desire occasion; that wherein they glory, they may be found even as we. For such are false apostles, deceitful workers, transforming themselves into the apostles of Christ. And no marvel; for Satan himself is transformed into an angel of light. Therefore it is no great thing if his ministers also be transformed as the ministers of righteousness; whose end shall be according to their works."

2 Corinthians 11:10-15

So we see, God is not mocked. Whatever a man sows, he shall reap. God is not going to harvest the tares. Satan sows the tares in the church, but at the end of the age, God has a harvest. When you see that the harvest is ready, you can distinctly notice the difference between the tares and the wheat.

In just the same way that God sees the tares and the wheat, God can see the prideful and the humble. Wheat manifests humility, and tares represent the prideful. God resists the proud and gives grace to the humble. The humble go to heaven and the tares are plucked and bundled and thrown into the fiery furnace. So it is that the tares and the wheat have grown together. It is hard to distinguish one from the other.

At harvest time, the wheat starts to bow over just like a sign of humility. Tares stick straight up. So shall it be in God's harvest. Now is that time. Look around. God is about to manifest every worker of iniquity, every false prophet. You will distinctly know the difference between the tares and the wheat. It is all about the heart. Get rid of all the leaven out of you as well. Fall on the rock or the rock will fall on you and crush you to pieces. God is going to have His people--- the easy way or the hard way. We cannot become like the Pharisees and Sadducees of old. Pride manifests blindness. That is why the Sadducees were "sad you see" because they couldn't see Jesus right in front of them.

{ WHAT WINE ARE YOU SIPPING? }

God showed me that in the life of a believer there will be people around you, or come around in the circle, that if they don't have an intention of giving up this life, they can speak something to you that could direct you to a self-centered intention because they don't want to go where you and God want you to go. Jesus was telling his disciples and preparing them for persecution, preparing them to walk in His glory, telling them that He had to suffer and to give his life. Then Peter, out of selfishness and lack of revelation, directly after such an awesome revelation, spoke out of that wrong intention, wrong spirit. Then in the next breath, in **Mark 8:31-38**, after being so prophetic, he was so pathetic, trying to misdirect Jesus with his soulish desires not to be led where God wanted him to go, to the Cross. Jesus even called him Satan. Beware of those who speak around you that might sound so good. They speak of the easy way to walk in the Glory, to do whatever you want, not what God wants, because they fight against submission, counsel, truth. These are spots in your feast. God has Joshua groups all over nations that are about to cross over and that are getting ready to go where no man has ever gone before. An Apostolic vision is God's vision. If you don't get involved in God's Vision, the only thing that will happen because they don't want to go is DE-vision, because it's too hard for them to surrender themselves, to move in the power of God and fullness of Joy. Before joy and true peace is righteousness first. God will keep them in the wilderness. They will die there. New wine is new ways of healing, doing Kingdom realms of Glory. Old wine counsels and confuses with opinions and self-ambitions. New wine has the answers. Old wine operates in the letter, much teaching never coming to the knowledge of the truth. New wine becomes the word. Old wine gets sourer in religion and tradition. New wine becomes better and better in the presence of its maker. Old wine operates in fear of the letter. New wine operates in kingdom power and demonstration of the good news. The old wine is in a debate. New wine has all the answers. Old wine studies and serves the logos. New wine has ears to hear what the Spirit is saying. Old wine is always trying. New wine is doing. So what wine are you drinking? Whose teaching are you hearing: the anointed voice of Christ, or the voice of Eli, or your own voice? Watch those with their seducing prophecies and fleshly ambition. That will keep you in the wilderness! Testimony: I have never been in as much freedom and joy and the lack of Lucifer's voice than I am now! **Hebrews 5:8.** Jesus learned obedience through what he suffered! What you suffer on the outside brings Glory on the inside. Don't believe the lying spirit that wants you to build your kingdom in the wilderness, but let God build you a fortress on the rock in the Promised Land. Follow us as we follow Christ.

IN A HOUSE

In a house, there are vessels of honor and vessels of dishonor. God is saying, "Shane, this is the season that I'm going to unveil the tares from among the wheat. I'm cleaning my house. I will have a time of revealing every hidden motive and agenda of man's heart." The funny thing is that tares never bow first. Look at the wheat when it is harvest time. The wheat bends over and the tares stick straight up. It stays high and lofty. In fact, a harvester has to bow down to pick and see the harvest. Tares are always seen, and they do not bow to the system of the Kingdom. That is the kingdom of love and selflessness. The Lord warns us of such evil workers.

"Beware of false prophets, who come to you in sheep's clothing, but inwardly they are ravenous wolves. You will know them by their fruits. Do men gather grapes from thorn bushes or figs from thistles? Even so, every good tree bears good fruit, but a bad tree bears bad fruit. A good tree cannot bear bad fruit, nor can a bad tree bear good fruit. Every tree that does not bear good fruit is cut down and thrown into the fire. Therefore by their fruits you will know them." Matthew 7:15-20

When the Lord speaks of a false prophet, He is not only talking about someone with a title that is off on prophecy. He is not only talking about someone who claims to be a prophet and is not. He is talking about anyone who says he is a man of God or a Christian, but what he spews out of his mouth is his own opinions, not by the spirit of God. Prophecy means to speak forth. False means fake, wrong words, or not true. For example: Rev. Jesse Jackson spoke forth that Barack Obama was the Joseph that God has raised up to save this country. He went around to places that would receive him. He said Barack Obama is God's man. He was not speaking the Word of God but his own agenda, his own plans, not the Word of God. He claims to know God - this is one type of false prophet. The Bible says that if you do not love your brother, how can you say that you love God whom you do not see? True prophets speak truth in love, but they speak truth. Today, truth is very rare. When you find someone who speaks it and speaks it in volumes, keep connected to them. They will tell you the truth even if it will cause them to be persecuted, lose friends, or family. Whatever the price is, they will pay it. These are God's sheep and true prophets. Wolves look like sheep, they smell like sheep, talk like sheep, but they are not sheep. They are among us, but they are evil workers, never allowing God to do a work in them. They follow the desires of their own heart. This is the season. Jesus is the reason. God is going all out to expose darkness and those who are being deceived. He loves all, even the wolves and the tares.

God is exposing, shining His light in an effort to make them a vessel of honor prepared for the master's use! His main use is to make us harvesters who are righteous from the inside out. Wolves are more self-righteous than righteous which is a filthy rag to God. Here are some signs for wolves:

. They are always right, and everyone else is wrong.

. They have a hard time submitting to authority.

. They are critical in spirit.

. They will always find fault in someone else but never judge themselves.

. They chase after precious stones but not after the pearl of great price: Souls.

. They will not let others speak into their lives.

. They hear from God about themselves and will only let God tell them.

. They are rarely at peace with themselves or others.

. They lack the fruits of the spirit and easily walk in the flesh.

. They become distant from the pack because they need to hide.

. They do not want anyone to see what they are hiding.

. They are always concerned about their own needs before anyone else's.

. They are satisfied in their own self-righteousness.

I can go on and on. We all fall short in every area. God is working on us, but wolves have already arrived in their own mind making them very prideful.

We all are in the process of deliverance, and God is going to show the difference. This season, there is a change coming, a discerning of spirits like never before. True prophets will be known by their truth not by their title or their name, pointing people to Jesus not themselves, and God will back their words with the fire and the power of God with miracles, signs and wonders. God is putting His structure back in form. Every manmade ministry and self-promoted ministry will come down. The House of Esau is going to be revealed, and the house of Jacob, the House of fire, will be established in the land.

The harvest is here. The workers are few, but God will be promoting many and demoting many. Do not be shocked. What you see is God and not the devil. He is cleaning his house, all the filthy, all the religiosity, all the control, the manipulation, the fleecers, He will get rid of! Mark my words: Change is coming, already bearing fruit and producing new wine.

"For the time has come for judgment to begin in the house of God; and if it begins with us first, what will be the end of those who do not obey the gospel of God?" 1 Peter 4:17

Put on your tunic and robe, Sheep - not judging people but judging the spirit that is controlling and deceiving them. We will never judge any man. That is God's job and His alone, but He will allow you to test the spirits, to see if they are of God.

"Nevertheless the solid foundation of God stands, having this seal: "The Lord knows those who are His," and, "Let everyone who names the name of Christ[a] depart from iniquity." But in a great house there are not only vessels of gold and silver, but also of wood and clay, some for honor and some for dishonor. Therefore if anyone cleanses himself from the latter, he will be a vessel for honor, sanctified and useful for the Master, prepared for every good work." 2 Timothy 2:19-21

So continue to search your hearts and let God purge everything that is not put there by God — a soul cleansing - and do not take any offense or record of wrong done to you. That is a stronghold that the Devil uses to stop the power and purging of God, the vileness in the depths of our souls that wants to say, "It's all about me." No. It's about Jesus. Jesus alone. The kingdom of God is at hand. In this next passage, we can see what is already happening right now:

"Therefore judge nothing before the time, until the Lord comes, who will both bring to light the hidden things of darkness and reveal the counsels of the hearts. Then each one's praise will come from God." 1 Corinthians 4:5

See? God is shining His light onto every hidden motive and every agenda of the flesh. Now is that time. This needs to be our portion.

"Therefore, since we have this ministry, as we have received mercy, we do not lose heart. But we have renounced the

hidden things of shame, not walking in craftiness nor handling the word of God deceitfully, but by manifestation of the truth commending ourselves to every man's conscience in the sight of God." 2 Corinthians 4:1-2

This is that: The first shall be last. God is taking us back to the foundation – the Rock – Jesus – the simple gospel with power and demonstration of the Holy Spirit. Not with enticing words of man but with truth, love, joy. In Him, we have all sufficiency and no lack of any good thing. Search your heart before He has to do it. Fall on the rock before the rock falls on you. He will not let you go – His beloved. He says, "I long to be with you. Clean your house. A house divided cannot stand. Sweep it. Clean it." "Show yourself approved, and I will do mighty exploits through you. Let my word become flesh in you. I'm getting you ready for the time to come, as spoken in **Matthew 24**. Those who understand will see."

"But we have this treasure in earthen vessels that the excellence of the power may be of God and not of us. We are hard-pressed on every side, yet not crushed; we are perplexed, but not in despair; persecuted, but not forsaken; struck down, but not destroyed." 2 Corinthians 4:7-9

WARNING TO ALL FALSE VOICES AMONG US

Who has sat in the council of the Lord? Who has the word of the Lord? Many are speaking just as in the days of old. Baal had his prophets; God had his prophets. God has and is raising up true voices to guide His people in these last days. There are many false prophets in the church as well as the world. These prophets run around bestowing imaginations of their own heart, performing witchcraft before your eyes. God has his Elijahs in place. Scripture tells us. God even warns His people about following after such.

"And the LORD said, "Because they have forsaken My law which I set before them, and have not obeyed My voice, nor walked according to it, but they have walked according to the dictates of their own hearts and after the Baals, which their fathers taught them," therefore thus says the LORD of hosts, the God of Israel: "Behold, I will feed them, this people, with wormwood, and give them water of gall to drink. I will scatter them also among the Gentiles, whom neither they nor their fathers have known. And I will send a sword after them until I have consumed them." Jeremiah 9:13-16

Church, this is not a game we are playing. God is not mocked. He is His word. Quit running after a man to tickle your ears. God is saying to put first things first. Anything that is on your mind more than God and His covenant plan is an idol. It can be a job; it might be football; it might be sin in your life. God loves you so much. The enemy hates you so much. God chastens those He loves. Now is the time to hear the words of the Lord. God speaks about it.

"Thus says the LORD: 'In this manner I will ruin the pride of Judah and the great pride of Jerusalem. This evil people, who refuse to hear My words, who follow the dictates of their hearts, and walk after other gods to serve them and worship them, shall be just like this sash which is profitable for nothing." Jeremiah 13:9-10

Before the USA election for president in 2008, many voices were crying out with a righteous tongue; however, many followed the false prophets. Now we see the results of this error. Deception came in all forms. Truth is truth. I warn all of you false prophets who call yourselves prophets that God will judge every idle word. You have said, "The Lord says...," but He never spoke it. God has me warning you now. Stop telling people what they want to hear, preachers and prophets alike.

"For both prophet and priest are profane; Yes, in My house I have found their wickedness," says the LORD. Therefore their way shall be to them Like slippery ways; In the darkness they shall be driven on And fall in them; For I will bring disaster on them, The year of their punishment," says the LORD. "And I have seen folly in the prophets of Samaria: They prophesied by

Baal And caused My people Israel to err. Also I have seen a horrible thing in the prophets of Jerusalem: They commit adultery and walk in lies; They also strengthen the hands of evildoers, So that no one turns back from his wickedness. All of them are like Sodom to Me, And her inhabitants like Gomorrah. "Therefore thus says the LORD of hosts concerning the prophets: 'Behold, I will feed them with wormwood, And make them drink the water of gall; For from the prophets of Jerusalem Profaneness has gone out into all the land.'" Thus says the LORD of hosts: "Do not listen to the words of the prophets who prophesy to you. They make you worthless; They speak a vision of their own heart, Not from the mouth of the LORD. They continually say to those who despise Me, The LORD has said, 'You shall have peace'; And to everyone who walks according to the dictates of his own heart, they say, 'No evil shall come upon you.'" For who has stood in the counsel of the LORD, And has perceived and heard His word? Who has marked His word and heard it? Behold, a whirlwind of the LORD has gone forth in fury—A violent whirlwind! It will fall violently on the head of the wicked. The anger of the LORD will not turn back Until He has executed and performed the thoughts of His heart. In the latter days you will understand it perfectly. "I have not sent these prophets, yet they ran. I have not spoken to them, yet they prophesied. But if they had stood in My counsel, And had caused My people to hear My words, Then they would have turned them from their evil way And from the evil of their doings. "Am I a God near at hand," says the LORD, "And not a God afar off? Can anyone hide himself in secret places, So I shall not see him?" says the LORD;" Do I not fill heaven and earth?" says the LORD. "I have heard what the prophets have said who prophesy lies in My name, saying, 'I have dreamed, I have dreamed!' How long will this be in the heart of the prophets who prophesy lies? Indeed they are prophets of the deceit of their own heart, who try to make My people forget My name by their dreams which everyone tells his neighbor, as their fathers forgot My name for Baal. "The prophet who has a dream, let him tell a dream; And he who has My word, let him speak My word faithfully. What is the chaff to the wheat?" says the LORD. "Is not My word like a fire?" says the LORD," And like a hammer that breaks the rock in pieces? "Therefore behold, I am against the prophets," says the LORD, "who steal My words everyone from his neighbor. Behold, I am against the prophets," says the LORD, "who use their tongues and say, 'He says.' Behold, I am against those who prophesy false dreams," says the LORD, "and tell them, and cause My people to err by their lies and by their recklessness. Yet I did not send them or command them; therefore they shall not profit this people at all," says the LORD." Jeremiah 23:11-32

"Then many false prophets will rise up and deceive many." Matthew 24:11

"Now he who received seed among the thorns is he who hears the word, and the cares of this world and the deceitfulness of riches choke the word, and he becomes unfruitful."

Matthew 13:22

Because of your lust and imaginations, you have brought quick deception to your country and to the world. True prophets will allow themselves to die to bring the truth to a people. What greater love does one have than to lay down his life for his brother? You preach love, false love, seducing God's people with a seducing tongue, not warning them about the danger of not walking in righteousness, using the grace of God in vain. How dare you! Jesus is the only way. Repentance must happen. You have changed the Bible to preach your books; watchmen who don't watch, seers who can't see; prophets who prostitute your gifts for fame and fortune. God is warning to you. Repent, repent, repent!

"Beware of false prophets, who come to you in sheep's clothing, but inwardly they are ravenous wolves." Matthew 7:15

Jesus warns us about these prophets. He is speaking to the church.

"Blessed are you when men hate you, And when they exclude you, And revile you, and cast out your name as evil, For the Son of Man's sake." Luke 6:22

"Woe to you when all men speak well of you, For so did their fathers to the false prophets." Luke 6:26

God through Peter will seal this word and warning to you. Anyone who knows the Lord holds to His saying:

"But there were also false prophets among the people, even as there will be false teachers among you, who will secretly bring in destructive heresies, even denying the Lord who bought them, and bring on themselves swift destruction. And many will follow their destructive ways, because of whom the way of

truth will be blasphemed. By covetousness they will exploit you with deceptive words; for a long time their judgment has not been idle, and their destruction does not slumber."

2 Peter 2:1-3

"But these, like natural brute beasts made to be caught and destroyed, speak evil of the things they do not understand, and will utterly perish in their own corruption, and will receive the wages of unrighteousness, as those who count it pleasure to carouse in the daytime. They are spots and blemishes, carousing in their own deceptions while they feast with you, having eyes full of adultery and that cannot cease from sin, enticing unstable souls. They have a heart trained in covetous practices, and are accursed children. They have forsaken the right way and gone astray, following the way of Balaam the son of Beor, who loved the wages of unrighteousness; but he was rebuked for his iniquity: a dumb donkey speaking with a man's voice restrained the madness of the prophet. These are wells without water, clouds carried by a tempest, for whom is reserved the blackness of darkness forever. For when they speak great swelling words of emptiness, they allure through the lusts of the flesh, through lewdness, the ones who have actually escaped from those who live in error." 2 Peter 2:12-18

God is not mocked. If you sow corruption, you shall reap it. Watch in the next couple seasons. God will be bringing some well-known ministries out of circuit. Some will disappear, but don't be shaken. They have had plenty of time to repent, but did not turn to Him. God will turn them over to the destruction of their flesh but will save their soul.

{ 12 CHARACTERISTICS OF A FALSE PROPHET }

1) FALSE PROPHETS: They prophecy future events, but they don't come true. TRUE PROPHETS: None of their words hit the ground.

2) FALSE PROPHETS: They call themselves prophets. TRUE PROPHETS: Others call them prophets by the fruits of the gift.

3) FALSE PROPHETS: They seek the gifts. TRUE PROPHETS: They seek the giver with all their hearts (not double agents).

4) FALSE PROPHETS: They keep people worldly focused. TRUE PROPHETS: They set people apart from the world.

5) FALSE PROPHETS: They are very charismatic (entertaining Spirit, dramatizing, soulish). TRUE PROPHETS: They are serious, bold as a lion, and righteous (spiritual).

6) FALSE PROPHETS: They dance around Jezebel's table. TRUE PROPHETS: They call out sin.

7) FALSE PROPHETS: They esteem themselves better or higher than others. TRUE PROPHETS: They are lowly, meek, and humble.

8) FALSE PROPHETS: They make you the center of prophecy to create need for him or her. TRUE PROPHETS: They are

God-centered. They focus on His purpose and His plans for you.

9) FALSE PROPHETS: They go everywhere they can go. Bigger is always better. TRUE PROPHETS: They only go where God sends them.

10) FALSE PROPHETS: They slow down the meeting so everyone focuses on them and their gifts. TRUE PROPHETS: They give the word with fear, no matter who is listening or not.

11) FALSE PROPHETS: They say a lot of stuff (blah, blah, blah). They are platform Prophets speaking over the entire Body. Everything is hit or miss, and you don't really know what they said, but it sure sounds good. TRUE PROPHETS: They are direct and to the point.

12) FALSE PROPHETS: They draw people to themselves constantly. TRUE PROPHETS: They point people straight to God.

GOODBYE BABYLON, HELLO KINGDOM

We must come out from the hands of the task master into the hands of the potter. Slave. What is a slave? In this chapter we will surely see how God sees, and we will overcome the god of this world and his schemes. Through a dream, this message has been birthed. Get ready to begin to see with the eyes that are from above and begin to shake off what has to be shaken. Remember, whatever you trust in is your god. Whoever you serve is your master. Whatever you think, you become (**Prov 23:7**). This is why the Lord tells us to think on things above. Remember: Paul warns us about seducing spirits that creep into the church in the last days, seducing, enticing, or tempting. These spirits are to get you to focus on yourself, to focus on the things of this world. I realize that the pure word of God is not popular because it has nothing to do with flesh. It is spirit, and it is life. This is why the spirit of Babylon is in the church and in the world.

Many have become entangled. We must come out from among them and be separated. Did you know that holy means to be separated or consecrated? This is what the Bible says, BE HOLY. Be separated because I have separated you! In other words, I have made you separated and consecrated.

In my dream, it was a very notable speaker with one of the biggest television audiences and congregations, but they have become slaves of Babylon. We must first see what the spirit is saying. Secondly, we must start to make our way totally out of the world institution, Pharaoh's garden! There is a way that seems right to a man but in the end brings forth death (**Prov 14:12**). Anything that controls you is your master.

Here are two important contrasts:

WORLD + MONEY = POWER = EVIL = DEATH!

KINGDOM + MONEY = RESOURCES = SOULS = LIFE!

Everything is what you make it. Money in the hands of a sinner conceives more sin, a false state of well-being, and false security. Pride.

Money in the hands of a believer, a saint, conceives alms-giving, good works, and establishes the Kingdom of God on the earth. It is not sensual. It does not fill the need of the five senses. It fills the needs of the kingdom. So in this chapter we will bring a great divide. Come on, let's get to it!

WHAT IS A SLAVE?

1. A person who is the property of another, a bond servant.

2. Someone entirely under the dominion of another.

The plan of the Babylonian system is to make everyone slaves. If they own you, they will own your thinking. The plan of the anti-Christ deception is to own your house, your car, to own you, and then they will own your thinking. To do this in a free society, they must bankrupt or take over. The only way to do this is to destroy. This will happen again and again because the little god of this world, the devil, has a plan. If the banks own everything you have, and the government takes over, then they own you. Stimulus and a bad economy are being done on purpose to slowly numb a person into believing that their only hope is to trust in the enemy and to take their handouts until they have seduced you into totally depending on the government – the spirit of the world. God is allowing this, but that does not mean He condones it.

Hollywood is the heart of this spirit of Babylon over this nation, seducing you sensually. Remember: Everything in the Old Testament is a shadow of spiritual things, the Lord's voice by His spirit. Religion will tell you that Babylon is a place in Iraq. The spirit will tell you that it is in a man's heart. The Babylon spirit is a principality over regions and cities. It is the spirit of this age, the World. Example: New York is run by this spirit as well as Hollywood. It is the strongman, and as long as the strongman has dominion, all other kinds and principalities have full access, such as perversion, greed, and so on.

"Now the Spirit speaketh expressly, that in the latter times some shall depart from the faith, giving heed to seducing spirits, and doctrines of devils." 1 Timothy 4:1

Why is it in the church? Because of:

1) Compromise
2) False teachers
3) False prophets
4) Apathy
5) Selfishness
6) Idolatry

A little leaven leavens the whole lump. You see, sensuality is not just sex. It is the fleshly desires of the:

Eye – Sight

Nose – Smell

Ear – Hearing

Touch – Feeling

Mouth – Taste

How do we overcome? By his grace, love, obedience, trust.

"No man can serve two masters: for either he will hate the one, and love the other; or else he will hold to the one, and despise the other. Ye cannot serve God and mammon." Matthew 6:24

This is why the tithe and offering will break the altar of mammon. Whatever you put first is first, in mind and heart. This is broken by training and obedience.

Train up a child in the way he should go, and he shall not depart from it. The ways of the world are opposite of the kingdom, but the church is trying to serve both. This is impossible. When I say the church, I mean those who are not following God with all their heart. The bride is different.

"But seek ye first the kingdom of God, and his righteousness; and all these things shall be added unto you." Matthew 6:33

See, the World is not righteous.

"Consider the ravens: for they neither sow nor reap; which neither have storehouse nor barn; and God feedeth them: how much more are ye better than the fowls?" Luke 12:24
"A little that a righteous man hath is better than the riches of many wicked." Psalm 37:16

"And again I say unto you, It is easier for a camel to go through the eye of a needle, than for a rich man to enter into the kingdom of God." Matthew 19:24

Narrow is the way.

"But they that will be rich fall into temptation and a snare, and into many foolish and hurtful lusts, which drown men in destruction and perdition." 1 Timothy 6:9

Here is the kicker. Don't get me wrong. God wants us to have a lot of assets, but He must first get Babylon (the World system) out of us so that we are a pure channel. He will add everything we need, and MORE, but we must have our trust solely in Him. The wealth of the wicked is stored up for the righteous. Come out of Babylon. Have Him take Babylon out of us.

"Lay not up for yourselves treasures upon earth, where moth and rust doth corrupt, and where thieves break through and steal: But lay up for yourselves treasures in heaven, where neither moth nor rust doth corrupt, and where thieves do not break through nor steal: For where your treasure is, there will your heart be also. The light of the body is the eye: if therefore thine eye be single, thy whole body shall be full of light."

Matthew 6:19-22

Two things:

1) Unbelievers are carnally minded.

2) Wisdom for a believer would be to put things away where they would be for eternity, forever, not left for the things of sensuality.

"If therefore ye have not been faithful in the unrighteous mammon, who will commit to your trust the true riches?"
Luke 16:11

If he knew what his last day on earth would be, what would a believer do? He would sell everything and give it to God if he was free. If in bondage, however, he would still be consumed by self! We must live in account to God as if every day were our last. Then when our last day does come, we will be totally in right standing with Him.

"Whereas ye know not what shall be on the morrow. For what is your life? It is even a vapour, that appeareth for a little time, and then vanisheth away." James 4:14

What are true riches? Anointing, faith, power, revelation, abundance, peace, prosperity, wholeness, joy. These things money cannot buy. In these true riches, there is abundance of finances! Let's get the first things first and put away self and receive all that heaven has for us!

WITCHCRAFT WITHIN AND AROUND

Hearken to the voice of the Lord! God is saying we must submit to His Word, His government, and His ways. He is exposing what is true and what is a fraud. He is on a mission to sift and clean and purge His people. We must get our character in line. We must get our hearts set on fire, and we must become the Word and learn to flow in the Spirit. The rebellious will dwell in a dry land. Be hungry, be diligent, and be true to your first love. Submit yourselves to His statutes and guard your hearts with all diligence. Flee the enemy's camp. Now, run for your life. If you are hearing this message, you are truly blessed. We must purge ourselves from every form of religion. Move only in the spirit. Now, now, now! Know this: Rebellion turns into witchcraft. Witchcraft will be cut off. Look at our lives and the lives of those with whom you are in communion and flee to higher ground and purge yourself, now!

"Now Eli was very old, and heard all that his sons did unto all Israel; and how they lay with the women that assembled at the door of the tabernacle of the congregation. And he said unto them, Why do ye such things? for I hear of your evil dealings by all this people. Nay, my sons; for it is no good report that I hear: ye make the LORD's people to transgress. If one man sin against another, the judge shall judge him: but if a man sin against the LORD, who shall entreat for him? Notwithstanding they hearkened not unto the voice of their father, because the LORD would slay them. And the child Samuel grew on, and was in favor both with the LORD, and also with men. And there came a man of God unto Eli, and said unto him, Thus saith the LORD, Did I plainly appear unto the house of thy father, when they were in Egypt in Pharaoh's house? And did I choose him out of all the tribes of Israel to be my priest, to offer upon mine altar, to burn incense, to wear an ephod before me? and did I give unto the house of thy father all the offerings made by fire of the children of Israel? Wherefore kick ye at my sacrifice and at mine offering, which I have commanded in my habitation; and honourest thy sons above me, to make yourselves fat with the chiefest of all the offerings of Israel my people? Wherefore the LORD God of Israel saith, I said indeed that thy house, and the house of thy father, should walk before me forever: but now the LORD saith, Be it far from me; for them that honor me I will honor, and they that despise me shall be lightly esteemed. Behold, the days come, that I will cut off thine arm, and the arm of thy father's house, that there shall not be an old man in thine house. And thou shalt see an enemy in my habitation, in all the wealth which God shall give Israel: and there shall not be an old man in thine house for ever. And the man of thine, whom I shall not cut off from mine altar, shall be to consume thine eyes, and to grieve thine heart: and all the increase of thine house shall die in the flower of their age. And this shall be a sign unto thee, that shall come upon thy two sons, on Hophni and Phinehas; in one day they shall die both of them. And I will raise me up a faithful priest, that shall do according to that which is in mine heart and in my mind: and I will build him a sure house; and he shall walk before mine anointed forever. And it shall come to pass, that every one that is left in thine house shall come and crouch to him for a piece of silver and a morsel of bread, and shall say, Put me, I pray thee, into one of the priests' offices, that I may eat a piece of bread." 1 Samuel 2:22-36

"And the child Samuel ministered unto the LORD before Eli. And the word of the LORD was precious in those days; there was no open vision. And it came to pass at that time, when Eli was laid down in his place, and his eyes began to wax dim, that he could not see; And ere the lamp of God went out in the temple of the LORD, where the ark of God was, and Samuel was laid down to sleep; That the LORD called Samuel: and he answered, Here am I." 1 Samuel 3:1-4

"Remember therefore from whence thou art fallen, and repent, and do the first works; or else I will come unto thee quickly, and will remove thy candlestick out of his place, except thou repent." Revelation 2:5

"And the LORD said to Samuel, Behold, I will do a thing in Israel, at which both the ears of every one that heareth it shall tingle. In that day I will perform against Eli all things which I have spoken concerning his house: when I begin, I will also make an end. For I have told him that I will judge his house for ever for the iniquity which he knoweth; because his sons made themselves vile, and he restrained them not. And therefore I have sworn unto the house of Eli, that the iniquity of Eli's house shall not be purged with sacrifice nor offering

93

forever. And Samuel lay until the morning, and opened the doors of the house of the LORD. And Samuel feared to shew Eli the vision. Then Eli called Samuel, and said, Samuel, my son. And he answered, Here am I. And he said, What is the thing that the LORD hath said unto thee? I pray thee hide it not from me: God do so to thee, and more also, if thou hide anything from me of all the things that he said unto thee. And Samuel told him every whit, and hid nothing from him. And he said, It is the LORD: let him do what seemeth him good. And Samuel grew, and the LORD was with him, and did let none of his words fall to the ground." 1 Samuel 3:11-19

"A reproof entereth more into a wise man than an hundred stripes into a fool. An evil man seeketh only rebellion: therefore a cruel messenger shall be sent against him. Let a bear robbed of her whelps meet a man, rather than a fool in his folly. Whoso rewardeth evil for good, evil shall not depart from his house." Proverbs 17:10-13

Let's cry out!

"It repenteth me that I have set up Saul to be king: for he is turned back from following me, and hath not performed my commandments. And it grieved Samuel; and he cried unto the LORD all night." 1 Samuel 15:11

"And the LORD sent thee on a journey, and said, Go and utterly destroy the sinners the Amalekites, and fight against them until they be consumed. Wherefore then didst thou not obey the voice of the LORD, but didst fly upon the spoil, and didst evil in the sight of the LORD? And Saul said unto Samuel, Yea, I have obeyed the voice of the LORD, and have gone the way which the LORD sent me, and have brought Agag the king of Amalek, and have utterly destroyed the Amalekites. But the people took of the spoil, sheep and oxen, the chief of the things which should have been utterly destroyed, to sacrifice unto the LORD thy God in Gilgal. And Samuel said, Hath the LORD as great delight in burnt offerings and sacrifices, as in obeying the voice of the LORD? Behold, to obey is better than sacrifice, and to hearken than the fat of rams. For rebellion is as the sin of witchcraft, and stubbornness is as iniquity and idolatry. Because thou **hast rejected the word of the LORD, he hath also rejected thee from being king.**" 1 Samuel 15:18-23

Samuel the prophet told Saul what God wanted, but he decided to compromise.

{ WRONGS }

1) He thought he knew better than God.
2) He had a greedy spirit.
3) He was full of pride.
4) He continued on and got worse and worse.
5) His heart become more evil. He, at this point, allowed demons to torment him.

Read the book of **Jeremiah, chapters 5 through 6:15.**

"And it came to pass, when Joram saw Jehu, that he said, Is it peace, Jehu? And he answered, What peace, so long as the

95

whoredoms of thy mother Jezebel and her witchcrafts are so many?" 2 Kings 9:22

"Because of the multitude of the whoredoms of the wellfavoured harlot, the mistress of witchcrafts, that selleth nations through her whoredoms, and families through her witchcrafts. Behold, I am against thee, saith the LORD of hosts; and I will discover thy skirts upon thy face, and I will shew the nations thy nakedness, and the kingdoms thy shame. And I will cast abominable filth upon thee, and make thee vile, and will set thee as a gazing stock." Nahum 3:4-6

"And it shall come to pass in that day, saith the LORD, that I will cut off thy horses out of the midst of thee, and I will destroy thy chariots: And I will cut off the cities of thy land, and throw down all thy strong holds: And I will cut off witchcrafts out of thine hand; and thou shalt have no more soothsayers: Thy graven images also will I cut off, and thy standing images out of the midst of thee; and thou shalt no more worship the work of thine hands. And I will pluck up thy groves out of the midst of thee: so will I destroy thy cities. And I will execute vengeance in anger and fury upon the heathen, such as they have not heard." Micah 5:10-15

DANCING WITH JEZEBEL

JEZEBEL: Its main purpose is to shut down the prophetic voice in the church. When Jesus spoke in **Revelation 2:19-29**, He was speaking to the leaders of the church because, as the anointing runs from the head down, so does the entrance of unclean spirits, such as Jezebel. Its main purpose is to control the leaders so God cannot move through His body. It wants to grieve the Holy Spirit. When this spirit comes into the church, it has the leaders teach on the Jezebel spirit and tricks the people so that everyone starts to look at each other to see if they have some characteristic of that spirit. Then walls are put up.

The leaders become consumed, and this beast becomes more powerful. Unity and freedom will kill this giant, but first repentance must come from the head down. Leaders are responsible to bind and loose this beast, but when they let it in, the heavens become brass. This spirit will come and seduce leaders. It is not concerned about the sheep. If it can take out the head first, then it automatically takes out the body.

It knows the damage. It will do it from the top. We must cover one another, but cover our leader first. In the Old Testament, Jezebel wanted to destroy the prophet Elijah (**1 Kings 19:2**). In the New Testament, the same happened to John the Baptist. They asked for his head (**Mark 6:24**). So if Jesus Himself has rebuked the church for the Jezebel spirit in Revelation, and the Old Testament is always a shadow of what is to come, watch out for false fire: Controlling pastors and leaders who will always be content to be the only voice, the only teacher, the only one prophesying. Watch out! As anointed as this leader might be, this leader might be dancing with Jezebel!

DANCING WITH JEZEBEL

Part I

Church, God sent me halfway across the country to see this spirit in full action (but this is happening everywhere). The first night, the eyes of my spirit were shut. He will always work around any obstacle to touch and reach His children. He sent me there while I was in the wilderness. Now I know why God led me to the wilderness: To send me to this church that is possessed by Jezebel, and they had no idea. The second night, at this revival meeting, God put my seer's eyes on fully, and what I saw was atrocious. The next morning, during the pastor's breakfast, they took me on several tours trying to convince me that I should move there. I felt like I was at Disney World on one of those timeshare tours. They wanted to show me how beautiful and how big their golden calf was and why I should give my life for it.

I'm going to expose Jezebel and Ahab, how they work hand and hand, and how witchcraft is produced from this spirit. When I arrived in the Midwest, the first night, God gave me all these dreams. I was very confused. I thought, "God I just got here and now you're showing me all this stuff." I understood that if He had shown me before I went, I would have thought He was giving me a sign not to go. So, He waited.

He is a lot smarter than I am. Don't get me wrong. God is moving at this large fellowship. Remember: Jesus in the book of Revelation was speaking to the churches - to the seven churches. Five of them had one major problem.

Correct. Jezebel is plaguing the American church. We have seen many books about unmasking Jezebel in the marketplace. What I have realized is that many of them have good points, but they are incomplete because they are written from a leader's perspective only, so it is biased. Yes, the season is here. God is going to use many to expose darkness and those who are allowing these things because of love for the Body. Wake up, Church. This is what Elijah was born to do. Many Elijahs are coming out of the cave. They will no longer shy back. God will back His Words. Truth has to be spoken. God is raising up His remnant. No one that manipulates God's sheep will be tolerated any longer.

The remnants are more concerned about pleasing Him rather than pleasing man. They are not here trying to make people like them. We are all called to move in the gift of prophecy, but the true prophets of God will be displayed.

Many have gone out and prostituted this gift, and now they are using it for money and for fame, and the spotlight has captivated them. Even many notorious prophets all over Christian television are being deceived and are now giving many false prophecies. Are they God's children? Yes. Are they anointed? Yes. Do they move strongly in the gift of prophecy? Yes. Are they true prophets? Only they and God know. No. You also can know through the spirit of discernment. Test the spirits (**1 John 4:1**).

Remember: True prophets do not have a new word every week. They are seasonal and bring a word of correction and adjustment, and this word is from the heart of God. They do not move that strongly in the edification gift as the entire body can. They suffer; they cry; they labor for a word; and when they birth it, it is not always the happiest thing - but it is pure truth. You don't practice being a prophet. You are one. Yes, God will take years to cultivate character, timing, and maturity, but the Word is true.

Imagine Jeremiah now - just a little boy. "God, I can't do that!" He didn't practice it. He spoke for God. It didn't happen after 10 years of reading books about dreams and visions or going to prophetic conferences. How about Samuel, this little boy? God spoke. He had a message for Eli. Eli was letting things go on in God's house. The deaf get deafer. See the difference between the gift and the office? I just wanted to lay the foundation. It's the same for every prophet in the Bible. They are a messenger of God with no room for error. Many were not received and many got stoned and killed, not because they were false prophets, but because they told the truth and exposed the intentions of the hearts of nations, kings, and groups. I had a sequence of dreams around eight months ago on a very well-known minister. I am not going to expand on that, but I will tell you that in the last days we need to keep ourselves unspotted from the world. God says that if we sow corruption, we shall reap corruption. The Bible also says that pride comes before a fall. The one-man shows are over. God is about to unleash such an uncovering of all the garbage in the mainstream church: All these false teachings on prosperity, all those bling-bling ministries, the gold dust addicts, the diamond seekers, chasing after manifestations like drug addicts trying to find their next fix. How about chasing after the pearl of great price? (**Matthew 13:45**) The ones Jesus died for. Souls! That's when the supernatural will explode.

Those are the diamonds that God wants you to chase. I am not saying God did not do those manifestations or that He did. I think it is awesome, but signs and wonders need to follow you. Don't chase them. Chase God. Signs are for unbelievers to believe! I'm talking about the ones chasing them and the ones promoting them in order to build ministry names. We will go back to promoting Jesus. Now on the Jezebel topic - this topic is so deep and subtle but devastating. It creeps in little by little. It takes over the entire body from the head down. What you get out of it is a golden calf, a big building, or a couple books with your big picture smacked on the cover.

Remember: The gifts and the calling are without repentance. Jezebel promoted the prophet of Baal - Elijah promoted God, and they had a showdown in the book of Kings (**1 King 18:19**). I see a showdown on the horizon.

God will win as usual. The first thing this beast will do is try to shut down the prophetic voice or the prophets.

God brings the prophets to help a pastor, and they see the prophet as trouble because, yes, they want to do work for God, but they also want to have a big congregation. They want everyone to work for free to build *their* dream. They say, "God told me...," but the prophet says, "God wants you to do this..." So, there are two ideas: One = manly vision; the other = Godly vision. Then the beast creeps in.

The pastor doesn't see it because he is not a seer. Also, his heart is not totally pure so then Jezebel has found a place. It starts to seduce these pastors or leaders with lusts, and they start making a little rule here, a little rule there. They call it protocol.

They say we need to protect the sheep. No one is to lay a hand on anyone. No one is to prophecy to anyone except the ones whom we allow. This is not the Body of Christ. This is Jezebel. Yes, God shows up but He cannot move freely. My Bible says to prophecy one to another and to let others judge. How do we all learn and grow in the deep things of God and test the spirits? How can we test spirits if no one can talk from God? Not in the Jezebel church. Then these leaders have their own visions with the lust of the flesh and the pride of life mixing together.

What they start to do is to promote their own vision and to put a burden on the sheep. It's up to them to help, and many work long hours never receiving a penny for their labors, just an accolade once in awhile. So everyone has a job in this organization. It is run just like the world. The pastor leaders are untouchable. You need a special meeting just to talk to them. They always enter the room or congregation late and leave early out the side or back door while the action at the altar is still going on. Some leave with their entourage of armor bearers. Please, read this insight from my wife, Marlene, called *"Give Me Your Armor Bearer's Feet."*

When surely my Bible says, **"The first shall be the last and the last shall be first,"** Mark 9:35. What happened to being the doormat, the servant of all? Leaders are supposed to serve people more than anybody else, but they demand to be served instead. They have their two o'clock tee time. They have an assistant that wipes their sweat because they are so anointed and preach so hard. It's Jezebel. Their followers even start to dress like the leader, wear their hair like their leader. When they talk to the congregation, they put condemnation that they need to do more - not to win the lost – but to build their golden calf. They tell you that you are serving God and how pleased God is with you, never giving you a dime for your time.

Scripture tells us in **Luke 10:7, "For the laborer is worthy of his hire," and in 1 Timothy 5: 18, that the laborer is worthy of his reward.** They have a picture on the wall of the leaders, and they all have new cars and houses, mostly paid off, of course, by you who are working for them for free. Not only are you working for free - your tithe is paying for their house.

Note: The reason God is exposing this beast is that His children are bound and controlled and cannot grow into their Kingdom's assignment. They never grow up and become what God has ordained for them to become. They are not productive kingdom dwellers!

{ Give Me Your Armor Bearer's Feet }

By Marlene H Roessiger

There's nothing wrong with serving, but everything wrong when we treat ministers differently than our other brothers and sisters in Christ. I felt that there was something that God wanted to reveal to me so I went to my Strong's Concordance and looked up the words "servant" and "to serve." I was amazed when I found out that the "armor bearer" of the church of the New Testament is no longer a servant of one man, but a servant unto all. Paul, the Apostle, in his "great" position and recognition in the Body of Christ, said, **"I have made myself a servant unto all, that I might gain the more," 1 Corinthians 9:19**. He encouraged us to esteem others better than ourselves, according to **Philippians 2:3**. Peter also taught that we need to submit to the elder but also to be subject one to another (**1 Peter 5:5**) because every part of the body is supposed to receive the same, exactly the same, honor. He also told us to honor all men in **1 Peter 2:17: "Honour all men. Love the brotherhood. Fear God. Honour the king."**

This is a command to everyone - not only for the church to honor the ministers but for the ministers to honor the whole body of Christ. In **Galatians 5:13**, we read that we should serve one another: " **For, brethren, ye have been** called unto liberty; only use not liberty for an occasion to the flesh, but by love serve one another."

Back in the Old Testament, I saw the armor bearers serving the King, and in the New Testament, I saw a KING serving servants. It is written that JESUS took upon himself the form of servant in **Philippians 2:7: "But made himself of no reputation, and took upon him the form of a servant, and was made in the likeness of men."** He showed us that a great leader has to be a great servant. I can imagine Jesus telling the Old Testament's armor bearers: "Hey, stop doing that. I came to serve you, not to be served". **"For even the Son of Man did not come to be served, but to serve, and to give His life a ransom for many." Mark 10:45.** The word SERVANT is a forgotten word among the church leaders today (also among the brethren in Christ). Maybe I need to clarify...in the Body of Christ there is one Head. Christ Jesus is Lord of His body. (**Colossians 1:15-18**). No human being dare to take that position. Only Christ is the Head. All the rest of us are in the class Jesus spoke of in **Matthew 20** - servants!

Jesus taught His disciples, future church leaders, how to be the last, not the first, how to serve all, not some. He said in **John 12:26, "If anyone serves Me, he must continue to follow Me to cleave steadfastly to Me, conform wholly to My example in living and, if need be, in dying and wherever I am, there will My servant be also. If anyone serves Me, the Father will honor him."** Right after this passage, Jesus, the King of kings, the Lord of lords... **"laid aside his garment, took a towel, He poured**

water into a basin and began to wash the disciples' feet.." John 13:4,5. Peter couldn't understand why. "Lord, are my feet to be washed by you?" he said. Jesus answered, "You do not understand now what I am doing, but you will understand later on." I pray to the Spirit of wisdom and revelation to make the "later on" to become "NOW". Let NOW be the hour of revelation of this Word.

"So, do you understand what I have done to you? You call Me the Teacher and Lord." Or would we say, priest such and such, pastor such and such, apostle such and such, evangelist such and such, prophet such and such, teacher such and such, minister such and such, elder such and such? "You are right in doing so, for that is what I am." We are supposed to give honor to whom honor is due. "If I then, your Lord and Teacher (Master), have washed your feet, you ought (it is your duty, you are under obligation, you owe it) to wash one another's feet."

"Then he said, "Do you understand what I have done to you? You address me as 'Teacher' and 'Master,' and rightly so. That is what I am. So if I, the Master and Teacher, washed your feet, you must now wash each other's feet. I've laid down a pattern for you. What I've done, you do. I'm only pointing out the obvious. A servant is not ranked above his master; an employee doesn't give orders to the employer. If you understand what I'm telling you, act like it—and live a blessed life." John 13:13-17

Let us take off our garments, our very nice suits, and start to wash somebody's feet. Let us tell the Old Testament's armor bearers that it's over. Now the king will be the servant, and the servant of one man will be the servant of many. Let all of us take some towels and start to wash someone's feet. If anyone serves Him, if anyone loves Him, if anyone loves others more than themselves, let him follow Jesus. Let's prefer to serve rather than to be served.

My brethren, let's take a towel and wash some feet.

Marlene H. Roessiger

15

DANCING WITH JEZEBEL

Part II

Jezebel's function is to control. How? It controls with words and manipulation while you are vacuuming and dusting off the golden calf, I mean, God's house. God's house, they always say. That is how they get you to labor for free. My Bible tells me that serving God is growing up into what God has for you, your gift and assignment. This spirit keeps everyone IN the building. This congregation is the best one in the world, and everyone else should be here. The body never grows spiritually. They are children tossed to and fro because they are getting whatever the pastor tries to serve but no meat. Remember: I am exposing Jezebel--- not coming against any child of God, or His beautiful bride, but against the spirit that my Lord is telling me to reveal through these dreams and visions.

In the book of Malachi, it is written: "Will a man rob God through His tithes and offering?" The Jezebel Spirit makes you the thief when God is talking to the priest, the leader of the church, because everyone brought their tithe to the storehouse, the church building. The priest – the leaders - were spending the money and eating the goods. They were not taking care of the poor and the widows. This spirit will twist God's words and manipulate the sheep, never allowing the gifts in the House to operate. Many times, it moves through the wife of the pastor first, just like Eve – the Devil has no new tricks. Ahab, that is, the pastor, does most of the talking and preaching, but if you went to their home, you would see the wife making all the decisions for the church yet always lifting her husband up in front of the congregation. There are always silent rules and do's and don'ts, such as, "Don't leave your seat." This spirit loves to assign seats for people. The usher tells you where to sit, where to park, when to scream, when to rush to the altar, and it looks free because it has life, and God does show up. Now, let's get to how this spirit seduces through luxury and vanities when you go to these places.

Everyone talks about how awesome the leader is. Little Jesus, big leader. They even make you feel like you have a demon if you don't act like them. Don't try to go to the bathroom during the service. They will say, "You can't sit still because you have a religious spirit."

This spirit of Jezebel commits adultery with the system of the world and demands respect when we know that God's kingdom is opposite from the world system. God said that this spirit is seducing and teaching His servants. The church of Thyatira represents the world or religious system that allows anointing to make covenants with worldly systems (**Revelation 2:18**). Example: Voting for a candidate because of the stimulus that you would receive because of your charitable organization's status (or 501c3), so that in your own mind, you justify that God wants this because He needs to do this work. The whole time, this candidate goes against every moral law and law of God. This spirit will always justify its action in the name of God. They do outreach or have missionaries, but their heart is not in it, just to say we are doing this and that. They have a million dollar ministry and twenty thousand dollars a year for outreach. Ezekiel explained it like this: the branch up the nose.

And He said to me, **"Have you seen this, O son of man? Is it a trivial thing to the house of Judah to commit the abominations which they commit here? For they have filled the land with violence; then they have returned to provoke Me to anger. Indeed they put the branch to their nose." (Ezekiel 8:17).**

No matter what the leaders say – they are right and no one is allowed to question it because, of course, God tells them alone about the building, the golden calf. Luxuries, waterfalls, vaulted ceilings, coffee latte machines, bookstores, TV ministries and glass elevators, you name it, but people are starving in the churches and in the Third World countries. This spirit justifies itself because, remember, $20,000 out to missions, $200,000 for the pastor's salary. This is the sickness that we need as a body of Christ to stand up to and say no.

We are taking God's church back for God, for the lost, and for His freedom to move through all His children. Take these superstars off their thrones and put God back on the throne. You prosperity preacher, I warn you from God. You live by the dollar bill, and you will die by the dollar bill.

Every Kingdom built by the hand of a man-- you have labored in vain. You have been building your own kingdom and you are the top dog, the big CEO. Say good-bye. Repent, for God is bringing forth His remnant. Maybe you are the wicked that have been storing up the wealth for the righteous. Hand it back to God, to the poor, to the hurting. The Bible says that with the abundance of the heart the mouth speaks. That is why you always talk about money, telling people to give on credit so that God will erase your credit. Liars, thieves, fleecing the sheep. Paul said in **2 Corinthians 9: 7 — "Every man according as he has purposed in his heart, so let him give."**

Not grudgingly or out of necessity; not under compulsion, for God loveth a cheerful giver. Does it sound familiar to what you hear on TV? —Run to the phone quickly – slow obedience is disobedience. Or, "Someone out there...You are about to go bankrupt. Sow this thousand dollar seed on your credit card." And this guy has never shown you a video of outreach or why he needs the money, but the entire time, he talks about his car collection, about how he gave 58 dollars to get 58 blessings. How about this: "Now it's 2010. God said - ten people are going to sow 10,000!" For what?

God is about to reveal this spirit like never before.

"Love not the world, neither the things that are in the world. If any man loves the world, the love of the father is not in Him,

for all that is in the World, the lust of the flesh and the lust of the eye and the pride of life, is not the Father, but is of the World." 1 John 2:15-16

"You adulterous people. Don't you know that friendship with the world is hatred toward God? Anyone who chooses to be a friend of the world becomes an enemy of God." James 4:4

You yoke up with unbelievers turning the House of God into the House of Dagon and idols (**1 Samuel 5**). What happened to the sayings of Jesus? He said in **Matthew 20:25-28: "But Jesus called them to Himself and said, —You know that the rulers of the Gentiles lord it over them, and those who are great exercise authority over them. Yet it shall not be so among you; but whoever desires to become great among you, let him be your servant. And whoever desires to be first among you, let him be your slave— just as the Son of Man did not come to be served, but to serve, and to give His life a ransom for many."**

Who do you think you are? Get off of your high horse! Divorce Jezebel. Clean your church. Smash your golden calf. Repent and start to serve God's people. There are several churches in this nation and all over the world that have become night clubs full of people dancing with and dating Jezebel. God says, "I'm jealous." "I'm love sick." **Ezekiel 8**. Return. Return. Return. Time is short. Fun and games are over. God is taking back His bride from every Harlot. Release your control and your manipulation. God will reveal you openly. You have had many warnings in the night

113

visions. Do not lie. Boldness comes from God. This region will be God's, not man's. Loose, loose, loose! Face God, change your ways. Empty promises. Your words have become powerless. Repent and return to your first love or I will remove my candlestick from you, says the Lord. **Revelation 2:1-7**. If you are bothered by this word, ask yourself why and turn to God and live.

To the corrupt church:

"And to the angel of the church in Thyatira write, These things says the Son of God, who has eyes like a flame of fire, and His feet like fine brass: —I know your works, love, service, faith, and your patience; and as for your works, the last are more than the first. Nevertheless I have a few things against you, because you allow that woman Jezebel, who calls herself a prophetess, to teach and seduce My servants to commit sexual immorality and eat things sacrificed to idols. And I gave her time to repent of her sexual immorality, and she did not repent. Indeed I will cast her into a sickbed, and those who commit adultery with her into great tribulation, unless they repent of their deeds. I will kill her children with death, and all the churches shall know that I am He who searches the minds and hearts. And I will give to each one of you according to your works. —Now to you I say, and to the rest in Thyatira, as many as do not have this doctrine, who have not known the depths of Satan, as they say, I will put on you no other burden. But hold fast what you have till I come. And he who overcomes, and keeps My works until the end, to him I will give power over the nations—He shall rule them with a rod of iron; They shall be dashed to pieces like the potter's vessels—

as I also have received from My Father; and I will give him the morning star. —He who has an ear, let him hear what the Spirit says to the churches." Revelation 2:18-29

Note: The reason God is exposing this beast is that His children are bound and controlled and cannot grow into their Kingdom assignment. They never grow up and become what God has ordained for them.

16

HOUSE OF AHAB

Twelve years ago, I had an encounter. I said, "What is it, God?" I know I am called. The Bible pages turned supernaturally right to **Ezekiel 2**. He said who hath known there is a prophet among them be not dismayed. In **Ezekiel 2**, speak to the house for they are a rebellious house. Speak my Words. Then all these years God has been holding and pouring things, but I have not been releasing names. Now this is the year that God is revealing names and ministries. Why? To save them; for the truth to come so God can send His spirit. God is not against His people. He is against the spirit they are coming in agreement with that is shutting down the power and anointing of God in the Church. People are not being set free, and it is all here in the Word. Now it is time to reveal. Judgment starts in the house of God – God cannot judge America without judging the church first.

I am going to show you in black and white today. It's going on everywhere. That's why the spirit is growing. Now they are charging where they have never charged money before. I know a ministry who for years and years would have these huge meetings. It was a million dollars or more to do them, and every year they would take an offering and someone would come with $500,000, some would come with bits, big or small, and all of a sudden, in the end, paid in full God got glory, and they said God came through. Now they are charging money, the spirit of error and Balaam. Selling Jesus is wrong. Why is this more prevalent in America than in poor nations? Why would God not start doing that from the beginning? - The love of money. If it comes against the Word of God, it is doctrines of devils, philosophies of devils, motives of Satan, and agendas of man, which shuts down the Kingdom of God. You want me to go listen to somebody that is in error right in my face? How can I follow somebody that is not following the Word? There was grace for so long, but now God says, "NO!" We can make excuses all day, but it doesn't make it right. We can reason, we can say this or that. It says the wealth of the wicked is laid up for the righteous. We can go on all day with this, but there is a pure clean stream of the Word of God that is coming to the Church today. This is the time when the manifestation of the Sons of God will appear on the earth. God is setting order in His house. Period! The Spirit of Elijah, that is what He is going to do, draw the Sons of God back to the Father, the Father of Spirit, of truth and life, truth in love, so we can move in the power, and we can actually stop being offended at the truth and walk in it. I'll tell you this -Compromise is a lot more fun, because picking up your cross and denying yourself isn't just something you read. We need to live it. God's grace is sufficient to do it with us.

117

God has allowed me to get close to ministries then lets me see this stuff, and then He says get away. I start to get excited, and He says get away. God, why? He even lets me start to like things, and all of a sudden He opens my eyes. In Ezekiel, He puts a hole in the wall and God took him and says look through the hole, look at the defilements and all the things they are doing in the House of God, in my house. It was a seer anointing.

The Bible says if we know the truth about something and don't do it that it is sin with us. God is preaching truth, but we say, "Well, Jesus, we are under grace." That is the biggest deception ever because Satan has a foothold. Why would we give a place to the devil? Nothing can happen to us if we don't open the door. So we keep the door shut and humble ourselves under the mighty hand. Any Word, any doctrine, anything that exalts itself against the Word of God, we are to cast it down. So I cast down every lying spirit in the Church in the mighty name of Jesus. God is raising up a people who are so in love with the truth and the words of truth and the words of life that they won't be able to hear anything else. They will know that isn't God. A little leaven leavens the whole lump. God didn't say these things just because He is trying to say something. He said in the last days there will be doctrines of devils and seducing spirits creeping in the Church and will deceive many. You try to go to the deceived and tell them, but then you are told you are a legalist. All of a sudden they are smiling and doing everything, and one day judgment comes and everything is stripped when finances fall and the facade comes down in this country and everyone that depends on the beast here in this country. Then all of a sudden we're sorry, we will listen to you now. Yes, you're going to go through something, but God doesn't want you to. That is why God is bringing the Word.

Do exactly how He told you to do. Well, what commandments? If you love Him and obey Him and do His commandments to love, to speak the truth whether you are liked or not, God will reward you even in greater way. You say in your heart, "Well, you know they are not ready to hear that." What if they die tomorrow? When are they ready to hear the truth? Since when did the Bible have different levels: kindergarten, middle school, high school, and college churches in the Book of Acts? Some people have been there 30 years. Come on, where do we come up with that stuff? God says the truth is going to CLEAN you. That is why there is so much division because nobody wants to have the truth. The truth is the one that is going to bring the churches together. The truth is in His Glory. In John 17, it says they will be one as I am one for the Glory you gave them. I am telling you what; God's Glory is not going to rest in lying spirits.

Don't you know that every problem we have is backed by a spirit? It's not just people saying I want to be bad and I want to do this, and that's what God is using today to get this spirit out of the church. The Ahab leaders are becoming Anti-Christ and Anti-Word, and Jesus is the Word.

{ CURSE OF AHAB - SCRIPTURE EXPLANATION }

Omri was an idol (demon) worshipper and Ahab's father; Omri did worse than all the kings before him. He set the pattern for his son to follow and Ahab did evil in the sight of THE LORD above all that were before him, even Omri (**1Kings 16:25, 28 & 30**). He married Jezebel, daughter of Ethbaal (Baal worship), king of the Zidonians who worshipped Baal. So Ahab served and worshipped Baal. Ahab was influenced spiritually by Jezebel. Baal was the male god; Asherah – the female god (**1 Kings 16:31; 18:17-19**). Ahab told Elijah that he, not Ahab, was the one that troubled Israel.

Ahab would not take his responsibility but shifted blame for his problems and those of his father (**1Kings 18:21**). He persecuted the prophets (**1Kings 18:4,13,19**). Ahab told Jezebel about Elijah killing the prophets of Baal. Jezebel was the one that took action against Elijah, not Ahab.

Do you see who vowed to kill John the Baptist (**Matt 14:1-12**)? What Herodias was to Herod, Jezebel was to Ahab. Both Ahab and Herod were wicked, and in both cases the woman was more wicked. Both Jezebel and Herodias fostered hate that became deadly against a prophet of God. Jezebel hated Elijah and sought to kill him—Herodias hated John the Baptist, the New Testament Elijah, and succeeded in his murder. Seducing spirits are doing the same in church today, seducing the leaders to eat from her table, cutting off the voice (head) of the Prophets. With the seductive dance, came out a demonic hidden agenda. This truth is going to set the Church free.

He grieved over this. Ahab not only worshipped Baal, but he was disobedient to God because he didn't follow Elijah's prophecies. The Church today, they don't listen. They say that there are no prophets today, that it's Old Testament. They say that we can all hear God. Yes, you can, but God also speaks through people. He also has voices (messengers). He also has the spirit of Elijah that is coming, that is, one voice, one spirit that is going to restore the sons and daughters back to the Father in Holiness, and it is going to smash the altars of Baal and man and resurrect the Church, anointed and empowered and covered by the Holy Spirit and God. It stirs me up because they keep rebelling, and I know, God has shown me, there will be a great falling away when the shaking comes. It's here (when this country gets turned over). I am tired of going to nations to have to cast out demons out of all the leaders in the Church. It's time leaders don't have demons and people come in, and we don't have to cast demons out. The problem is America won't let the prophets in the Church to cast the demons out of their leaders. The head is most important.

His children were affected by the deeds of Ahab. He was dominated by his wife (Jezebel) to do evil and God forgave him when he humbled himself before God. Read **1 Kings: 21, 25, 29** He hated the truth and the Prophets of

God. Are you starting to see? He was willing to imprison and to torture them. Read **1 Kings 22: 8, 27**

You say that was Old Testament? Why did Jesus talk about all that in the book of Revelation in the New Testament? - Because He is giving us spiritual revelation. He is giving us deep hidden things to set us free and to strengthen His Church where the Apostolic Church is rising and the gates of hell will not prevail against it. That is why you are seeing so many altars resurrected in the Church, in America, and all over the world (Australia, California), Houses of Ahab, and dens of thieves.

We saw kids dancing in other nations and demons possessed them, and they think it is the Holy Spirit. What is going to stop all this? The truth is coming to clean up the Church, Elijah anointing, but as Jeremiah said, I am going to uproot and pull out everything that is not truth, and I am going to replant the truth. Who is God going to do that through? - Through His ministers and through His Holy Spirit.

{ AHAB CHARACTERISTICS }

He brought grief and judgment on himself and the nation. He opened the flood gates for idol worship into the nation and homes. He did not oppose murder for greed or any other purpose. Once entered into the mind of an Ahab man (Remember he was a king so God gave Him authority), he will accept more and more wanton acts of a depraved nature. There is a loss of manhood and fatherhood, castrating. Jezebel's aim was accurate in spiritual perspective;

her acts were against GOD and His plan. So by not opposing Jezebel, Ahab gave consent and is guilty of being an accessory to the crime with Jezebel. This is criminal! – Pastors and leaders are doing it today.

Satan's evil desires are seen in the evil acts of men (**John 8:44**). Influence is what a demon does to you from the outside; control comes from inside. Ahab broke ten commandments and coveted man's field. Ahab married a woman devoted to everything that God hated and forbid. The Church today is eating from tables of devils. The Church is married to everything in the world, the entertainment spirit in the world, fame and fortune, lust of the flesh, self-seeking, doctrines of self ambition, new age, self-motivation, lacking the Cross. When revival hits, millions of people will listen to this message and flee the House of Ahab.

Ahab married a woman devoted to everything that GOD hated and forbid. This opened a breach upon Israel through which Satan gained astonishing power and flooded Israel with evil. Even so, a man opposed to GOD who submits to his wife or other women, opens the floodgate for evil to pour upon his family and ministry.

{ AHAB REBELS }

The major rebellion was against GOD in Baal worship. He is a jealous God. Ahab went after other idols. Worshipping idols is the worst rebellion against GOD. Who else did that? Solomon, right? He had 200 wives, seducing spirits. Then what? The Queen of Sheba comes, and he ends up worshipping the Queen of Sheba's god. When he had a relationship with God, he got wisdom and favor from God. What do you think all these things are in the Bible for? For us just to say, "Oh, that was cool?" The Bible says in Ecclesiastes that there is nothing new under the sun, and it says in 1 John, 2 John, and 3 John that the spirit of the antichrist is in the world since the beginning. Satan is that; it's his armies; it's here today. We have all these false doctrines that think when we become a Christian that these things don't apply. It doesn't with Jesus but applies if we are seduced, and it says many are seduced in the Church. The Bible says seducing spirits will creep in the Church. They don't come and say, "I am the devil. Do you want me here?" Of course we would say, "No, get out," but they come in unaware. Then when you come and expose them, they say, "What are you talking about?" People are that ignorant, and the more they come and come, the more people are blinded. Satan blinds those that submit to him. Then they don't hear from God anymore. Then, all of a sudden, who is running the Church? - Satan, which is the Jezebel spirit. Jezebel actions are true sorcery. Rebellious Jezebel males and females will ask questions causing people to doubt their work and their ability to make decisions. Another motive behind the rebellion is wanting worship and the admiration. Elijah destroys Baals prophets. Read **1 Kings 18:17-40**.

That is why when I meet ministers, I ask them, "What do you want, a bunch of yes people around you to tell you everything you want - man idolatry? That is what they want, and they are called soothsayers! That is who Elijah killed. Who do you think God is going to take out when the Spirit of Elijah is in the Church in the last day, preparing the way of God, opening the clouds in the Church to meet Him in the air? He says in the last days I am going to send the Spirit of Elijah. It's right there in the Bible. The Spirit of Elijah is here. It's time.

Many times in deliverance demons inside will cry out for help. If the demon power is bound in Jesus name, the demons get out with no help. The name of Jesus answers by action - the demon leaves. Who is greater? Jesus is greater so we have the power and authority. We need to use it and get them out. God's people should be dictating direction and conditions, not Satan. God's people should be doing that. It is tough on Satan when there is an open display and he does talk to demons as long as it is hidden. He has power, but shown in the light of God, he limps away.

This is what happens...**1 Kings 18:28.** And they cried aloud, and cut themselves after their manner with knives and lancets, till the blood gushed out upon them. Satan cut himself, ate flesh and drank blood. The Devil usually will not exhibit himself when God's presence is real but will manifest when people give their will over to direction. The devil made me do it. Ever heard that? The devil didn't make you do it; you did it because you gave your will over. He will always lie. What did he say in the garden? You will not surely die, and there was some truth to that. There is always part truth. That's false doctrines that he is using to deceive believers, half-truth Gospel.

Now the most overlooked subject is Ahab's House, a designated leader. In **Isaiah** there is a picture of God's breakdown of God's order in the family and the Church.

"**And I will give children to be their princes, and babes shall rule over them. 5 And the people shall be oppressed, every one by another, and every one by his neighbour: the child shall behave himself proudly against the ancient, and the base against the honourable. As for my people, children are their oppressors, and women will rule over them. O my people, they, which lead thee, cause thee to err, and destroy the way of thy paths.**" Isaiah 3:4-5,12

This is a picture of the end times with a complete inversion of leadership. In the last two verses of the Book of **Malachi**, God emphasizes family order and Church order.

"**Behold, I will send you Elijah the prophet before the coming of the great and dreadful day of the Lord: And he shall turn the heart of the fathers to the children, and the heart of the children to the fathers, lest I come and smite the earth with a curse.**" Malachi 4: 5-6

How many know that judgment day will be great for those who know Him and who follow Him and believe Him, and it will be dreadful for those who don't know Him and call upon His name, Jesus, and be saved? So Malachi is talking about the Day of Judgment, the day of coming to be with the Lord. The Bible says to be absent from the body is to be present with the Lord. The dead in Christ shall rise first. All that is remaining will meet Him in the air and, boom, we will go right in front of the judgment seat.

126

Deliverance cannot be held unless we do according to the dictates of God's Word. This calls for a great deal of dying to self because of the nature of the society in which we live today. This all goes back to the assemblies for if we are not in order then society is out of order. Without order in the home there will be none in assembly. God is sending forth an Elijah spirit in these last days to bring order out of chaos. At the same time, the vicious Jezebel spirit was raging through Israel, and it is raging through the Church today. God sent an Elijah forth as was God's ways in those days. So God says in the last days I will send the spirit to return the sons back to Him in holiness and truth. It is today. The Elijah ministry is going forth in the land to offset the Jezebelic ministries, which have swept the earth. These two have always locked in bitter, clashing conflict. God will throw her to the dogs on the sickbed, and every Ahab and Jezebel and her eunuchs with her, in the hour of temptation that is coming on the earth. As we move deeper into the end times, this controversy will increase. There will not be peace and unity but rather a fierce battle for control in the home, in the church, and the nation. Before there can be a Jezebel, there must be an Ahab for Jezebel to take over. King Ahab had to abdicate and step down from His place of leadership. The great abdication means to renounce or give up your throne. This has come about by the failure of men who refuse to take the lead in families, leaders, and churches. The Church is allowing Ahab to be the head instead of the Holy Spirit, thereby violating Biblical principles in the order of the chain of command. Preaching or praising the Lord will do little unless we put it in practical applications in our lives, our churches, and our homes.

Ahab's life demonstrates principals to be avoided. Read **1 Kings 16: 29, 30.**

Why do men step down from their places of leadership? Over and over the problem has been men who abdicate leadership in their home, give up leadership, and want nothing to do with the Church.

A key reason is given in **1 Kings 16:31**:

"And it came to pass, as if it had been a light thing for him to walk in the sins of Jeroboam the son of Nebat, that he took to wife Jezebel the daughter of Ethbaal king of the Zidonians, and went and served Baal, and worshipped him."

The first principal operating in Ahab was that he considered the things of God trivial. How many today consider the things of God trivial, and why are you doing Halloween? Oh, come on, Brother, you are a legalist. It's trivial, it doesn't mean a thing; we can do a little sin here. We can do a little pagan. We can have Santa Claus, give everybody presents on Sunday. Or we can have the Easter Bunny hide eggs in the Holy place because you know God is grace and mercy. It's not a big deal. It is "trivial" to the false grace church, but it is a big deal to God. God's prophets can't stand it. We have this going on everywhere, and it is like no one is hearing God anymore. I am going to get the scriptures that prove everything I am saying right now. - And you see the false grace doctrines today and you looked on the sins of Jeroboam as trivial. The attitude that sin was not the problem freed him to do whatever he pleased because of fallacious reasoning. Ahab left the things of God to his wife and adopted even her religion. Heathen ways of paganism, holidays, women's liberation in American are all just another brick in the wall of the destruction of the family and was actually Jezebel taking her throne. Look at the time scale of the abomination that came right after the liberation movement and the morals that fell in this country when the woman wanted to do everything the man wanted to do in this country. Now they are letting them go out to the battlefield, and there is nowhere in the Bible that any woman should go to battle. The woman stayed home with the kids and the men went out to fight, and the man brought food home. Show me one place in the Bible where men brought their woman out to war with them. Now in America the women can be on the front line, and they fought for that just because of pride; that's all it is, and that is what Satan is: PRIDE, the spirit of perversion. He is the father of pride just sitting back laughing. Satan is against God's order. The government makes it impossible to live on one paycheck. Jezebel just got another notch, and it is another step to hell. The beast is rising but won't in God's church.

We see all the worldly ways and ideas, and we see the anti-Christ kingdom, the lying signs and wonders in the Church. We see miracle movies, all this stuff, and no truth. Satan can heal people. Satan can make you feel good. He can give you goose bumps, but he cannot move in power, and he cannot repent. Jezebel hates repentance. That's why she said she found no place of repentance, no place. She hates repentance. Satan hates people that repent so that starts getting taken out of the Gospel. Jesus talked about repentance all the time, maybe more times a day than He talked about anything. We hardly say that anymore. When Jesus comes, the Holy Spirit comes. He convicts us of all sin, and we run to the altar, and cry out, "God, save me from my wretched self!" That is what the Holy Spirit does, not take your prayer home to the closet tonight. You know you don't want to go to hell, so come on, just please say this prayer. Now by the power of God you said this prayer so you're not going to hell? Who dare tell them they are not going to hell? Either way is wrong. There is nothing that says automatically this person does this thing, does a back flip, and all these doctrines. I can go on with doctrines all day. Another doctrine of devils is to be spiritually minded is no earthly good. Jesus was the most spiritually minded man on earth, and He was the most earthly good man that ever walked the earth! We pick these things up from Jezebel all the time and eat from her table. We eat from her table! Well, he is the Pastor; he has a Church of 30,000. Who cares? Jesus had a multitude of people following Him when He preached the real Gospel. John says (in John 6:66) that the rest of His disciples walked with Him no more. Actually, if you have more people following you then the cross, probably neither you nor they are really following Jesus.

Everyone wants all the Churches to come together. I am telling you, get Jezebel out of the church and the churches will come together. Deliver Ahab and churches come together. They want to come together under the Anti-

Christ spirit that's head of the Apostasy. They are trying to leave everything in place and go do a citywide prayer meeting or a citywide baptism. Oh, we have to come together. Satan has to get out. If your church is full of demons, I am not going there, and I am not coming in agreement with it. Right? So God is not stupid. Of course, He wants us all together, but there is a way that seems right to a man but in the end brings forth death. They will say, "Brother, you are just a little guy, just come on man, just relax." So many people try to shut my mouth, and you know what? God is going to deal with them.

It is likely that Ahab married for convenience, lust, and political advantage, selfish motives. It is the same thing that is going on in the church today. We can receive from Pharaoh. Oh, Brother, go vote for that man, he is a liberal; he likes homosexual marriage, and we are going to get grants! It is that entitlement spirit, and we are going to vote because of what we can get.

We vote. I don't know, I mean do we vote anymore? I don't know - now you have to look to God. The Church of God is the only hope for this nation, Jesus is it. Jesus Christ, the power of His resurrection to transform lives and baptize us in the Holy Spirit. It's the only hope we have.

No movement. You can line up and can tape your mouth up for 20 years. Satan is the god of this world, and you can't go infiltrating the government. We do not fight flesh and blood. We fight on our knees in secret. You might work there, but take them aside and give them the truth. Seven mountains teachings, all these doctrines of devils are all up in the church. Then these big Babylonian conferences come and bring all these doctrines of devils. It is Jezebel and Ahab coming together for money. God is putting an end to it. This is the season. Jesus is the truth and power. The manifestation of the sons of God is going to appear, and it is going to come from the pure love of truth, and love and compassion for the lost and to heal the sick and to cloth the naked, to give when someone needed a drink when they were thirsty, and you were there for them. You just don't do that and don't even tell how to come to Jesus.

Jezebel was quite the woman; she painted her eyes and was heavily into sex for she was a priestess of Baal. Undoubtedly, she was beautiful, sensual, sexual, as well as this spirit is in the Church to compromise, to do spiritual fornication and idolatry. Like so many today, Ahab probably married for lust. Many today are coming to Jesus for what they can get out of Him. How does Ahab come? She wants the benefits, and she wants the compromise. Ahab got to be a man pleaser. We can't tell them that they will leave the church; that's it, you will become an Ahab. Let Jezebel come in and tell them everything they want. You have Ahab on TBN, God TV, everywhere, but you let anyone come in and prophesize false spirits, and you allow that spirit in - something that God has given you authority over – so you're an Ahab because God gives you leadership. If you as part of the Five- fold ministers that have allowed allow Jezebel and other teachings to come in, you have become an Ahab. Repent. That is what God is getting to in this whole thing. Just like in the home, watch this.

So many today, probably married for lust. Lust of what? - Pride of life! Now a guy is famous and has 50 armor bearers, and armor bearers are not even in the New Testament Church, and we say that is okay. Then some throw away the Old Testament. There is so much mixture and confusion out there. God is here to bring the truth. People come to God for all the wrong reasons. We see this right here: Marriage and relationship, people are plunging into marriage without counting the cost. People plunge to say the prayer of salvation not counting the cost, not knowing you have to give up everything, not knowing your life is not yours anymore, that you are to be transformed into the image of God. Anyone in Christ is a new creation, old things pass away and all things become new. You are not the same way. You are continuing to be changed and cleansed by the power of God. The Bible says the Holy Spirit will bear witness with our spirit that we are the Sons of God, and the Holy Spirit will mortify the deeds of our flesh. Jezebel does not mortify the flesh, it feeds the flesh. Ahab lets it happens because he was given the authority.

Ahab values are upside down. Isaiah charged that he called evil good and good evil. This is one of the biggest problems in the church today. Verse 31 states that Ahab's servants were following Baal to follow after other gods.

The next step is degeneration. There must always be an altar for them somewhere. This doesn't have to be a physical place but can be in the heart. An altar is a place of homage, respect, and influence, but, primarily, it is a place of input.

It is a place to let down all defenses and man's wisdom and philosophies, a place to open up and be receptive. Today there are new versions of altars of little gods: newspapers, recreations, hobbies, automobiles, and thousands of other things. Remember the Bible says Baal has 1000 faces. He'll come to you in 1000 different ways, 1000 different forms. It is Satan himself masquerading, even evil things come cartoon-like and, whatever, it's not a big deal.

God has called you to come out from among them and separate yourself, touch not an unclean thing. God says in the book of Revelation to come out of the spirit of Babylon, and He is talking to the church. Come out of her! Church, come out of Babylon! To follow after other gods is the next step down in degradation and there must be an altar. They erect it in people's lives. Such is a place of input that becomes our Baal and takes away from the true Almighty God and becomes a high place.

There is a spirit of the god of sports who rules over America weakening our families. The input into our lives, home, and children is not of God. It's funny that at super bowl, when you have the most people watching, you got the Baal worship; you got the worship of Madonna and Beyonce and Katy Perry doing all that demonic stuff.

Then in the American church, if it's super bowl Sunday, we either leave church early or set up a big screen, and then we allow the spirits in the church. You know Jesus is grace so we can do whatever we want now because He gave us a license to sin - NOT! It says in **Jude** that they'll turn the grace of God into lasciviousness, even denying their Lord, Jesus Christ. It's all in the Bible, but we hear these philosophies, the seven steps to this and the nine keys to that. Then all we need is the truth and the spirit to witness and the Holy Spirit to baptize us. Many people are told they are baptized, and they don't even know Him or have been baptized in the Holy Spirit. That is what is going on. Deception is rampant. It's in the Bible for the last days. We are not coming into agreement, but God has warned us in the last days. That is what got all the prophets killed. Man wants to do what man wants to do. What killed John the Baptist? He exposed the sin of Herod. Herod was alright with it. His wife was like, "Oh!" That made her look stupid, and he was sleeping with another one. Did John do that or was it his zeal? Nobody knows. If he kept his mouth shut it would have saved his life. Half the prophets, if they would have shut their mouths, would still be alive today. Right? If you shut your mouth, you will get more fame, more money. Jesus said you killed and stoned the prophets before you, and you are going to kill me, too. Your fathers were empty tombs! Father vs. Devil. You know all this yet you have no relationship with the truth. We need to say YES to Him. I am not going to be an Ahab. I am not going to be a Jezebel. I am going to love the truth. It is joyful to have time to be with the Lord. There is a separation going on and many people are going to be separated with the goats. They love God, but they love not the truth. What did God do? He said that He was going to turn you over to a reprobate mind. That means your mind will think like it is doing right. He said the blind lead the blind not into Glory but into the ditch. He was saying in Jeremiah about the pastors of end times, you scatter the sheep. It's all in the Word. So then in the last step, you say the Old Testament has nothing to do with us today. There were no churches in the Old Testament where they are called Pastors. Everything He says about the spirits in the Old Testament come in. So what do you do? You look at the attributes of these men and women that God says there are spirits on them. Look at Ahab, his character, ways, agendas, and so on; same with Jezebel, same with Balaam. If Jesus says these here, He means in the spirit, how the enemy used them. So that spirit is the same familiar spirit that will be on people today.

"And he reared up an altar for Baal in the house of Baal, which he had built in Samaria. And Ahab made a grove; and Ahab did more to provoke the Lord God of Israel to anger than all the kings of Israel that were before him." 1 Kings 16: 32-33

Ahab provoked the Lord to anger, above all the other kings before him. Why? Because God gave him Kingship. Man wouldn't have fallen in the garden if it said, "Oh, Eve seduced Adam." The demon seduced Eve, and then Adam said okay. Ahab spirit right there! Instead of saying, "Nope!" He would have said, "Woman, what did you do? Put that down," and went to God and said, "I stand before you and cover my wife." He would have forgiven her.

God would have said go on. God knew all that. He wants us to have relationship with Him. He wants us to multiply. He wants us to have choices. He created Lucifer

136

who fell and now is Satan. He has demise. God could have tied him to the pit. He let him loose on the earth for a reason. He didn't want robots. He wants us to have choices: That we are not going to choose Jezebel, not to choose Ahab, not to choose Satan, but that we are going to choose Jesus and all His righteousness. The reason Satan is on the earth is because God gives us a choice. God did it all. We come back into the garden when we come into relationship with Him but not if we are hearing everything that God tells us to do and we don't do it. He says the rebellious dwell in a dry land, and I call it the land of Nod. With Cain and Abel, He said to Cain, go into this dry land. He did not kill him. It was his punishment. Many Christians are in the wilderness because they allow Jezebel to feed them. They are getting fed by Jezebel. Then they get all these spirits, and they get the entitlement spirit. If the Ahab leader gives authority to the enemy, the church gets seduced.

Then God is talking to us about Amos. Amos is the last day Church. Some people will say that is Israel, but Israel did not have revelation back then. When God talks to us and uses these things, they are talking about the Church. The scriptures I want to use now is this:

"And I will turn your feasts into mourning, *its coming*, and all your songs into lamentation; and I will bring up sackcloth upon all loins, and baldness upon every head; and I will make it a mourning of an only son, and the end thereof as a bitter day. Behold, the days come, saith the Lord God, that I will send a famine in the land, not a famine of bread, nor a thirst for water, but the hearing the words of the Lord: And they shall wander from sea to sea (Sea represents the people from

people to people) from the north even the east, they shall run to and fro to seek the word of the Lord, and they will not find it." Amos 8:10-12

Remember before John the Baptist, in Malachi, it was 400 years supposedly there was no Word of the Lord. Elijah's time.

"Now I praise you, brethren, that ye remember me in all things, and keep the ordinances, as I delivered them to you. But I would have you know, that the head of every man is Christ; (*We are talking about Christ. Jesus had to be the head of the Church, not Satan, not smoke machines and laser lights, and entertainment*) and the head of the woman is the man; and the head of Christ is God. Every man praying or prophesying, having his head covered, dishonoureth his head. But every woman that prayeth or prophesieth with her head uncovered dishonoureth her head." 1 Corinthians 11: 2-5

Now look spiritually the part that says " Dishonoureth her head". Who is the head? CHRIST – Jesus, the Word. We have been dishonoring JESUS as the head of all things. Everything is out of order. It's not supposed to be tough to serve God and lead people. The only thing tough is the long suffering that we go through but there is a reason. It is not that God wants to push women down; He wants to raise them up. He wants to exalt them. He helps women to become all they are created to be. Satan knows they will never become what God has created them to be.

"A bishop (*overseer***) then must be blameless, the husband of one wife, vigilant, sober, of good behaviour, given to hospitality, apt to teach." 1 Timothy 3:2**

In the Church, if Satan comes in the Church, it will never do what God created it to do. In that aspect he is going to lose because God is going to have His Church, and the gates of hell will not prevail against it. Jesus is the bread of life and those that love Him will follow after truth and righteousness, and you are going to see it.

The five wise and the five foolish virgins (**Matthew 25:1-13**): Five were full of truth and the others of something else, themselves, doctrines of devils, conferences, paying man, getting false prophesies, letting people tell them everything is okay when all hell is breaking loose all around them, and they need to repent.

What do you think the oil is? The oil is the truth. The light is the truth. They had no truth. Jesus said the Church is like the ten virgins and five of ten will be foolish because they didn't love the truth. They lacked hunger. They were apathetic, worldly, not separated. Once you know the truth the Bible says the truth will set you free. That is why God is getting the truth into the Church, through the back door, the side, through this, through that, books, whatever. He is going to get the truth out. God says He is going to catapult. He is going to give money for TV, and revival is going to hit, and everyone is going to repent. Just like Satan will have everyone on TV and media bowing down and taking the mark of the beast. It's coming. Thank God we are hearing the truth today.

"For if the woman be not covered, let her also be shorn: but if it be a shame for a woman to be shorn or shaven, let her be covered." 1 Corinthians 1:6

Look spiritually, Guys. We have Ahab leaders allowing the gates of Hell to open in the church, the Anti-Christ spirit shutting out the true prophets. God says there are mysteries in this Word. Every religious person says, "Oh that is religious." Oh yes, but when God opens our spiritual eyes, puts on eye solvent, He shows us the spiritual dynamics of the Church because, remember, He says I am not talking concerning the man and woman, but I am talking concerning Christ and the Church. Spiritual, Guys!

"For the man is not of the woman: but the woman of the man. Neither was the man created for the woman; but the woman for the man." 1 Corinthians 11; 8-9

We are created for Jesus. Jesus wasn't created for us. Everyone has their own Americanized Jesus, Hollywood Jesus. Jesus isn't like that. Jesus hates this: Jesus doesn't want you to dance in Hollywood half naked because you are going to win people to Jesus. They have their own making up how Jesus is, leaving out righteous Jesus. Anything that exalts itself above God we are to cast down. That's what the Bible says. So you come to me with your opinions, great! I don't have time for that. Come with the Word of God and show us, and I will hear you. Opinions are everywhere. I think this: I don't care. The Word says this, walk in it. If you don't know the Word you better come in relationship with it because it is Jesus.

Jesus says I will give you the Spirit of Truth. He will guide you in all truth and there will be no error in truth. So the Holy Spirit is inside of us, and He has promised to guide us in all truth, to be our comforter, our helper. The only time we shut Him down is when we become rebellious. When we like so much more what the flesh wants to give us, and we say, "Well, not for now, later maybe," or then those people do not say anything, but they don't make a step to get in love with the truth, to let themselves get fed by the truth, what do they end up? Empty lamps. Jesus spoke of it. I'm telling you, just because you have great worship, God promises to inhabit the praises of His people. You can go to a Jehovah Witness meeting and praise God and the Spirit of God can show up. It doesn't mean anything. Paul says I do not come with man's enticing words and man's wisdom but with demonstration and power. For this cause, Jesus is manifested on the earth.

"For as the woman is of the man, even so is the man also by the woman; but all things of God. Judge in yourselves: is it comely that a woman pray unto God uncovered? Doth not even nature itself teach you, that, if a man have long hair, it is a shame unto him? But if a woman have long hair, it is a glory to her: for her hair is given her for a covering. But if any man seem to be contentious, we have no such custom, neither the churches of God." 1 Corinthians 11: 12-16

Paul was saying things that he didn't even know. God was going to bring revelation. He said there were mysteries not even being revealed. The other ones didn't even get the mystery of the Bride like Paul got it. Paul didn't even walk with Jesus. It was the spirit of wisdom and the spirit of revelation, and it was the Holy Spirit that anointed and baptized him apostle to the nations. Finally, Paul did more for God than the others, and, finally, they said Paul must be one of us.

"Giving thanks always for all things unto God and the Father in the name of our Lord Jesus Christ; Submitting yourselves one to another in the fear of God. Wives, submit yourselves unto your own husbands *(think of the Church now)* **as unto the Lord."** **Ephesians 5:20-33**

"Well," you say, "Jesus is the truth." But you also say "Well, you know it's not that bad. It's just a little leaven. It's just a little pagan stuff, and it's not going to hurt anybody." Then what comes in with that is the spirits that are doing it and the spirits that birthed it. Do you see it? That thing is dancing with Jezebel. That is why you see no power. Then all of a sudden there is an explosion of miracles. Jesus says there will be lying signs and wonders in the last days. We don't follow signs and wonders. We follow the truth. Jesus said an adulterous generation will seek a sign. The only sign He will give is the sign of Jonas. He was talking about when He was resurrected and the power.

Submitting one to another in the fear of God.

"For the husband is the head of the wife, even as Christ is the head of the church: and he is the Savior of the body." Ephesians 5: 23.

We can't have doctrines leading us and teaching us in the Church, teaching us the prosperity Gospel where all we are seeking after is money because we are going to do so much for God. That's not what the Gospel is! The Gospel is to transform us into the image of Christ, not into the benefits of Christ. There is so much compromise. All these people love God, and they are following God. Seducing spirits, things that just tempted Eve. Eve got tempted, others get tempted. Now they have temptation. Now they are charging for conferences whereas before they always went by faith because of the deception of money. Now they are doing this, now eventually everyone will start to charge. So you start to charge for conferences, and no one needs to give to God or to hear God anymore because there is a fee. Everything you do in the Kingdom is a fee. Deliverance: $20.00 over here, a little over there. Where is that in the Bible? Where is charging for anything? Jesus said freely give, freely receive, freely receive, freely give (**Matthew 10:8**). Jesus said He is sitting on the high place. He gave gifts to men for the edifying of the body of Christ so that we will all come to the full stature and measure of Christ. The measure of Christ, so the gifts are not ours, they are His. We are stewards of it. So we are prostituting our own God. I'm seeing yoga churches popping up. The Lord rebuke you, Ahab. Do you think God is going to be okay with that? They believe it because Jezebel is telling them, and they are surrounded by people in Jezebel. Ahab leaders are allowing her to seduce God's children. If you surround yourself with a bunch of voices that are against God, after some time you will eventually believe it. It doesn't matter if someone shook nations ten years ago. You have to discern and judge yourself and test the spirits whether they are from God, the scripture tells us. I am seeing so many major ministries falling left and right. It's spiritual fall and carnal churches can't see the fall. Blind lead blind. "That's okay. I am going to go to Hollywood to make some movies and be best friends with Oprah Winfrey, and I am going to keep my anointing dancing with Jezebel and eating from her table every day." Come on, Guys. Do not be unequally yoked with unbelievers.

Come out from among them and be separate. Separate yourself. That's a bad word nowadays. What about holiness? Be Holy for I am Holy. We don't talk about this anymore in the Church. It's all about what God can do for me. What can I do? God help me! Everyone needs help from God because they are all in disobedience, and all they need to do is repent and obey Him. The one-step program - the blessing comes through obedience. Repent, follow Jesus and follow His ways. It's really simple, but we will do 15,000 things, methods, or conferences trying to get you all around to that way when it is one step: Repent; follow His Word and His leading. Many leaders are going to die in the pulpit because God has tried to reach them so many times because they are leading the whole congregation the wrong way and then people will repent. When Ananias and Sapphira tried to corrupt the seed in the new Church by lying to the Holy Spirit, the fear of God came upon all. That's worse case of judgment over a church under God's grace! You go to the Church with a big offering and die. Wow! Show up to Church with a huge offering, it wasn't what I was supposed to fully give, but it was a lot of money, and come with an offering and die. We are talking about the Glory of the latter house shall be greater than the former house when in the book of Acts we don't even look at things like with the worms on the leader because he took the Glory of God (**Acts 12: 23**). Come on. Jesus was already resurrected! We don't hear this anymore because of Jezebel's teaching and feeding us everything we want to hear, strengthening our flesh, saying, "I am going to be something, I am going to be this, I am going to be that. I am going to have a woman pastor." You can be a co-pastor as a woman to your husband. It's Biblical that you can't be a single woman and lead a ministry. Satan is going to take you out. It is all the works of Jezebel. If you guys don't see it now, I don't know what else to tell you. It says the Lord loves the Church and gave Himself for her. You, as a wife, submit the same way. And your husband is going to give himself. The same way, the pastor is going to give himself to the people of God just like Jesus gives Himself to the Church. We need to come under His order. We want Jesus. I don't want any other spirits in my church. Boom, boom, that's the battle! Satan says, "I am going to take it," but God says the Church that He is building a Church and the gates of hell will not prevail. It is the Apostolic Church. So I am just waiting on it to happen, and I'm doing my part to bring it in, watching that these spirits don't affect me, believing that God will keep people around me with eyes that if I get off a little bit they will tell me, and, bam, with the fear of the Lord, they also will bring the Word without compromise holding back nothing from me! If I have to preach to one person at the end of the day, and that one person and I make it into heaven, oh well. We know that there are a lot more of us, but I am making a point. Praise the Lord. All I am accountable to do is what God's called me to do, and that's all you are accountable to do without compromising the truth. Compromise is full of leaven.

"For this cause shall a man leave his father and mother, and shall be joined unto his wife, and they two shall be one flesh. This is the great mystery." Ephesians 5:10

What's the mystery? Christ and the Church. She is coming out of the world.

"This is a great mystery: but I speak concerning Christ and the church. Nevertheless let every one of you in particular so love his wife even as himself; and the wife see that she reverence her husband." Ephesians 5: 32-33

Seek what God can give: Jesus, the Word! Don't seek what false doctrines can give you!

"One God and Father of all, who is above all, and through all, and in you all. But unto every one of us is given grace according to the measure of the gift of Christ. Wherefore he

saith, **When he ascended up on high, he led captivity captive, and gave gifts unto men.** *(Now that he ascended, what is it but that he also descended first into the lower parts of the earth? He that descended is the same also that ascended up far above all heavens, that he might fill all things.)* **And he gave some, apostles; and some, prophets; and some, evangelists; and some, pastors and teachers; For the perfecting of the saints** (*not for the deceiving of the saints*), **for the work of the ministry, for the edifying of the body of Christ: Till we all come in the unity of the faith, and of the knowledge of the Son of God, unto a perfect man, unto the measure of the stature of the fullness of Christ: That we henceforth be no more children, tossed to and fro, and carried about with every wind of doctrine, by the sleight of men, and cunning craftiness, whereby they lie in wait to deceive; But speaking the truth in love, may grow up into him in all things, which is the head, even Christ: From whom the whole body fitly joined together and compacted by that which every joint supplieth, according to the effectual working in the measure of every part, maketh increase of the body unto the edifying of itself in love. This I say therefore, and testify in the Lord, that ye henceforth walk not as other Gentiles walk, in the vanity of their mind, Having the understanding darkened, being alienated from the life of God** *(Imagine being in Church for your whole life and being alienated from God because your leader is being deceived.)* **through the ignorance that is in them, because of the blindness of their heart: Who being past feeling have given themselves over unto lasciviousness, to work all uncleanness with greediness. But ye have not so learned Christ; If so be that ye have heard him, and have been taught by him, as the truth is in Jesus: That ye put off concerning the former conversation the old man, which is corrupt according to the deceitful**

147

lusts; And be renewed in the spirit of your mind; And that ye put on the new man, which after God is created in righteousness and true holiness. Wherefore putting away lying, speak every man truth with his neighbour: for we are members one of another. Be ye angry, and sin not: let not the sun go down upon your wrath: Neither give place to the devil." Ephesians 4: 6-27

We see in **1 Kings 18, 19,** how they gave over to Jezebel. In the next chapter, I will talk more about Jezebel. Jezebel hates the word " repentance". Don't you know that the Bible says even Satan will dress himself up as a minister of light? You have to test the fruit. Jesus said test the fruit. I don't care how much money they have, how big the laser lights are, and how many followers they have. I am telling you Satan is getting a hold of many of God's elect this day. It is up to us to bear witness and to pray for them, bring the Truth to them, grab people, and show them the way. We are in a race, and we don't want to be left behind. Jezebel hates repentance. Ahab backs her. So we saw it in the garden with Adam and Eve. Now let's get to the last scripture. In **Revelation 2 and 3**, Jesus is speaking to the whole Church, but especially to the apostles and leaders of His people. Don't you know these things are the warnings before God starts breaking the seals, and all these things are opening up? I believe some of it is already happening.

Like it says in **Revelation 2:19-29**: I know your works. I know you are good men. I know your intentions are good. I know that you want to feed the poor. I know your charity, your service. I know all your faith, your patience, your works;

you want to be the last and not the first. Then God says, I have a few things against thee. He is talking to the Church now, but He is directing it to the leaders because you suffer that woman Jezebel, and now we found out all about her. Jezebel died years ago. Dogs ate her, right? So why would God say this, and how can you think that it is just a spirit because it says here she never repented? Spirits cannot repent. Satan cannot repent. His demons can't repent. This word is for whoever the spirit is using. Do you see that? It's right here. Boom, let the light come on.

Verse 20: "Notwithstanding I have a few things against thee, because thou sufferest that woman Jezebel, which calleth herself a prophetess, to teach and to seduce my servants to commit fornication, and to eat things sacrificed unto idols."

Someone will say that Ahab is trivial. We don't want to talk about Revelation, or we don't want to talk about Old Testament but do you see the importance of talking about these things? **"THAT woman Jezebel, which calleth herself a prophetess"**, you have allow her to teach and to seduce! You are letting her in the pulpit now, market-place ministry, making church into pyramids and business. She is bringing this in the church and gathering people from other churches. By not saying anything, you are saying it is okay, just like Ahab. If you are a prophet or if you are in the body of Christ and you see it and do not say it is not okay, then you become an Ahab. Jezebel is after the prophets. She is after everybody. Satan is after everybody. That is who the assault assignment is on. You see it with John the Baptist.

149

You see it with Elijah, right?

"**Jezebel calls herself**," that means God did not call her. God did not ordain her. God did not choose her or her teachings. She calls herself. She anoints herself. How many prophets, apostles, soothsayers call themselves? Here is my business card. I am prophet so and so, I am apostle so and so. Oh yeah, I went online for 25 bucks and got ordained. They have them all over, Facebook prophets. There are not as many prophets out there as you think, believe me. Many move in the gift of prophecy, but it is one of the nine gifts of the body of Christ that all can come under. There is a five-fold ministry gift. Then there is an office set in by God, government. It is a position, a standing, and an office. Every apostle is a prophet - every one of those that wrote the Bible and spoke forth for God, Paul, Peter. Paul desired that everyone would speak in tongues but even more prophecy (**1 Corinthians 14**). But not everyone that prophecies is a prophet and not every prophet is an apostle. An apostle is a builder, a man of order, and no one is talking about that.

Verse 21: "And I gave her space to repent of her fornication; and she repented not."

Remember demons can't repent. So this proves that this is a demon working through a person. **Verse 22: Behold, I will cast her into a sick bed, and all them** (*All the Ahab's with her. You are going to go with her if you are a leader.*) **I will cast them that commit adultery with her into great tribulation, except they repent of their deeds.**

Only people can repent. Angels can't repent. Demons

can't repent. **Verse 23: "And I will kill her children with death."**

When we give ears to her words, and start following them we become her children. We fornicate with her doctrine and teaching.

What? But some say "That's the New Testament; We are under grace". Brothers, the grace of Jesus is pure, holy and it has nothing to do with this deception of grace, the greasy grace. So how can we take only all the things we like from the Word and preach that to the people every week? That is deceptive as well.

Verse 23: "You shall know that I am he which searcheth the reins and hearts: and I will give unto every one of you according to your works."

"Father, we thank you for the truth, and open our eyes. We ask you to not let us be critical of others. Not to think we are better because we see. Not to give us self-righteousness. We ask to have meekness and cry out for our brothers and sisters. God, we ask for divine appointments that we could communicate Truth to them that they would be able to flee"

God is raising up a whole house of people that will affect a whole culture, a whole generation. God is opening up peoples' eyes, and people are coming to the light. You say, "Well, the Church is the light." Well, according to the Word and to the times that we are living in, it isn't. In the last days (this is the last days), He said the light was almost out, in the time of Eli as well. God raised up a Samuel. Eli never stopped hearing the Word of the Lord, and he let His sons fornicate with Jezebel, in the house of God. Now we have a spiritual house. He let them do whatever they wanted. See, Ahab will let you do whatever you want in the Church and in this temple called YOU!

This is real Word. This is the truth. Ahab is worse off than Jezebel and no one ever talks about him. Let's get to him first. He is the head. Let's expose the head and give the head chance to repent as well.

"So Father, I pray for every prophet, every pastor, every apostle that you have ordained in leadership that they will not be intimidated by the spirit of Jezebel and every husband that will not influenced or be taken out by the spirit of the age and the spirit of Jezebel. Father, we ask you for mercy. Father, your mercy triumphs over judgment. You love us and you love them, and that is why you want to bring us truth. You use the foolish things to confound the wise. Father God, help all rejection and all mocking and all word curses that come against your true voices that they will not be able to penetrate them anymore. God, that they will be dead for themselves and will be able to speak in the time of darkness and shine light, Your light, God, that you are going to release with the one voice, the spirit of Elijah. Father, we pray for the spirit of wisdom and understanding, the knowledge of You and Your Truth, God. Father, let them know that you are not trying to take anything away from us, but Father God, let them know that you are trying to cover us, you are love. Protect us and bless us. Bless us with the Kingdom of God and joy, righteous, and peace. You will give us peace in tribulation! We don't want to be turned over to tribulation because we have been disobedient sons and daughters of God. God, I pray for myself right now and everybody here. Any of us can be deceived right now. The Bible says that, if possible, even the elected one will be deceived (**Matt 24:24**). Everyone just get on your knees, and ask God to help you never to be deceived!"

Right now, it looks pretty nasty. And God said I will have a house, and it will be called a house of prayer, and you have made it a den of thieves. How can we have a house of prayer and be selling merchandise on the tables all the time? When did it become a marketplace? When did the Church become any less than a house of prayer for all the nations, a house to meet with God, a house to reverence God, a house to have a clean Word of God? It says in **Ezekiel 43**, they will defile the altars and pollute the altars, and that is what is going on. The thing that really bothers most of us that are getting the truth is that they don't hear it, and it really hurts us. Then they mock or talk behind backs bringing division because of a false revelation of Christ. If they do continue to do that, it is just pride, but God is plucking many out of the fire, plucking many out of deception. Even this day there will be hundreds plucked out reading this book and will begin to see. God wants to restore the Church. He doesn't want to have to shut down churches because they are overtaken by Jezebels, the seducing spirits of the world. He wants them to repent so He can bring them back to their first love and how He created the Church to be. We know from the scriptures

153

many won't do it. God is raising up a Church that is one Church, and the gates of hell will not prevail against it.

Concerning the real church of Christ, the remnant bride, when people come in one way, and they will leave out free, filled with the Holy Spirit, testifying, running from city to city, on fire for God, not trying to go to a conference to figure out seven ways to be blessed. You are already supposed to be blessed and the Church is supposed to raise you up into the stature of Christ. The reason we have schools and such is that half the churches are not in fellowship with God, and people that are hungry have to go to find something to eat. Come on, that is the truth. No one should have to go anywhere. There needs to be a place in every city, every region.

"Father, we give our ears, and we give you our hearts, Lord. Father, set us free today from anything that would keep us from you and your the Truth. We decree and declare that we will not tolerate Jezebel or submit to Ahab. Father, we thank you today, and we repent. We ask you, Lord, to keep us from being deceived at any level. You have good plans for us, plans to prosper us, for a hope and a future. We thank you for it, God. We thank you, God, that we can call you Papa and Daddy! We thank you that you will use us mightily, and it will not go to our heads. God, so many are being tossed to and fro. We ask you to continue to create the Father's heart in us so we will know who to lead, people who really want to know the Truth. Amen."

17

ANTI-WHAT? ANTI-WHO?
ANTI-ME? MAYBE YOU?

"He who says, 'I know Him,' and does not keep His commandments, is a liar, and the truth is not in him."
1 John 2:4

"Do not love the world or the things in the world. If anyone loves the world, the love of the Father is not in him."
1 John 2:15

This is a call to our brothers and sisters to repentance. Deception has been your bread. This word is for my brothers and sisters who continue to stand up and fight for darkness. Because of pride, you will miss the blessings that God has for you as you continue to stand for your vote.

To those around the nation, in the body or out of the body (only God knows), the body of Christ: Get in His will; make no alliance with the World. Now we have an administration that is not at all concerned with God, Jesus, or righteousness, but who lie and say they are.

"They went out from us, but they were not of us; for if they had been of us, they would have continued with us; but they

went out that they might be made manifest, that none of them were of us." 1 John 2:19

Many so called churches and leaders around America call themselves, "Reverend." God says, "Reverence Him and HIM ALONE," but some of these, "Reverends," continually fight for unrighteousness. They are of the synagogue of Satan.

"Little children, it is the last hour; and as you have heard that the Antichrist is coming, even now many antichrists have come, by which we know that it is the last hour." 1 John 2:18

The Bible says, "Many," so we can clearly say that anyone who makes laws to take Jesus out of this nation or to increase the murder of an innocent life is surely anti-Christ, as is anyone who takes away the sanctity of a man and woman in marriage. The devil wants everyone to focus only on the one, the dragon, when many are taking over the world and the church. Repent. Repent for voting the way of the anti-Christ and believing a lie. Line up.

"Who is a liar but he who denies that Jesus is the Christ? He is antichrist who denies the Father and the Son." 1 John 2:22

"And every spirit that does not confess that Jesus Christ has come in the flesh is not of God. And this is the spirit of the Antichrist, which you have heard was coming, and is now already in the world." 1 John 4:3

Take eye solvent. Wash your eyes and see. There are many antichrists among us: The leader in Syria – anti-Christ; the leader in North Korea – anti-Christ; the leader in Iran - anti-Christ; the leader in China – anti-Christ; the leader in Russia, the Czar – anti-Christ. Hitler was an anti-Christ; Oprah Winfred – anti-Christ. Guess what? Our own leader is an anti-Christ as well.

"Little children, it is the last time: and as ye have heard that antichrist shall come, even now are there many antichrists; whereby we know that it is the last time." 1 John 2:18

Don't argue with truth. Accept it and conquer it. Enter into the Truth.

Stop trying to find the one and know that there must first be many. These evil people are on a path for a one-world religion and a one-world government: This is what they call the New World Order. This is biblically to come, but cleanse your hands, and never again let the enemy deceive you. Stand up for your God and righteousness. The Bible says, "A double-minded man is unstable is all his ways." God is showing His people how they have been deceived and showing them the motivation of their hearts.

This anti-truth world order hates the Jew first, and guess what? They hate you - the Christian. Don't be yoked up with unbelievers. Infidels will deceive and lie to you and call you a hater because you won't go along with their false unity. As long as Satan is here, we will never have peace.

157

Don't believe a lie. This is not a color thing. This is a kingdom thing. The beast is already arising. This is a system coming out of the people. The water represents people in Revelation. The horns are the leader who will advance this beast. Then when it's time, the son of perdition will be known. I believe Satan himself will enter into this leader.

Anyone who doesn't have the light is against Jesus and is against Christ and is an anti-Christ. You do not have to listen to them when they will cause you to sin. Be a Daniel. Do not bow down to this system. You see how easily a large part of the church has been deceived. So don't think that you are so spiritual. Humble yourself. Follow His light - not your culture; not your uncle; not your auntie; nor your mother; but follow Christ – the light.

"Beloved, now we are children of God; and it has not yet been revealed what we shall be, but we know that when He is revealed, we shall be like Him, for we shall see Him as He is."

1 John 3:2

Cleanse your minds and your hands. Become a living word. Many are following the wrong leaders and people, even in their religious so-called churches. Jesus spoke of them as the synagogue of Satan, so if Christ is in you, you call a fox a fox. Don't be "Jezebeled" by them. Roar and watch things shift.

"Whoever abides in Him does not sin. Whoever sins has neither seen Him nor known Him. Little children, let no one deceive you. He who practices righteousness is righteous, just as He is

158

righteous. He who sins is of the devil, for the devil has sinned from the beginning. For this purpose the Son of God was manifested, that He might destroy the works of the devil."

1 John 3:6-8

If you have leaders telling you to do something unrighteous, get out from among them. The blind will lead the blind into a ditch, peddling their doctrines of self-indulgences, tainted with the leaven of the world, telling you to make unrighteous decisions based on their cultures or opinions. I'll add false teachers and false preachers. These heretics will have their portion with hypocrites.

"Beloved, do not believe every spirit, but test the spirits, whether they are of God; because many false prophets have gone out into the world." 1 John 4:1

Don't follow a title. Don't follow a man. Don't follow anything but the truth and the Spirit of truth. He will guide you into all truth. For the rest of us, continue to shout from the roof top, and don't come down.

18

ANTI-CHRIST SPIRIT IN THE CHURCH

"And every spirit that confesseth not that Jesus Christ is come in the flesh is not of God: and this is that spirit of Antichrist, whereof ye have heard that it should come; and even now already is it in the world." 1 John 4:3

"This then is the message which we have heard of him, and declare unto you, that God is light, and in him is no darkness at all." 1 John 1:5

This is the time, Church, the Devil has been working on us. Since the fall of man, when word got out to Pharaoh that a deliverer was coming forth to set the Jews free, Pharaoh decreed to kill all the first born. First, the natural, then the spiritual. **(1 Corinthians 15:46)**

Another example: Moses, a type and shadow of Jesus. Moses = natural deliverer / Jesus = spiritual deliverer

This is how it always is. "**And he said, When ye do the office of a midwife to the Hebrew women, and see them upon the stools; if it be a son, then ye shall kill him: but if it be a daughter, then she shall live." Exodus 1:16**
This Jesus – the King of the Jews – Herod got word of this king of the Jews, Jesus Christ our Messiah, coming

into the world. Again, Herod, led by an anti-Christ spirit, kills all the first born. **"Then Herod, when he saw that he was mocked of the wise men, was exceeding wroth, and sent forth, and slew all the children that were in Bethlehem, and in all the coasts thereof, from two years old and under, according to the time which he had diligently of the wise men." Matthew 2:16.**

Now, two thousand years later, the devil has not stopped his plan from the beginning. Now we have leaders that sign abortion bills, that allow murder of unborn and born children. The world is waiting for us, sons of God, millions of deliverers. Little Christs. So the enemy has a decree to kill, to abort, as many babies as he can to mess up the plans of God.

"For the earnest expectation of the creature waiteth for the manifestation of the sons of God." Romans 8:19

Now we have a leader just like Herod, just like Pharaoh and Hitler. They all had this spirit. This spirit is the world--- the world hates the light. Now we have socialist regimes because we wanted it. We wanted Saul. We, the majority, wanted these kings. The deception is that God put them in power. No, the devil is the god of this world. Because of our disobedience, God is just stepping back. Satan will be Satan.

"Therefore seeing we have this ministry, as we have received mercy, we faint not; But have renounced the hidden things of dishonesty, not walking in craftiness, nor handling the word of God deceitfully; but by manifestation of the truth commending

161

ourselves to every man's conscience in the sight of God. But if our gospel be hid, it is hid to them that are lost: In whom the god of this world hath blinded the minds of them which believe not, lest the light of the glorious gospel of Christ, who is the image of God, should shine unto them."

2 Corinthians 4:1-4

See, the devil is the god of this world. Most people don't acknowledge him or worship him physically or consciously. We do it through the lust of the flesh, the pride of life, and disobedience to the Word. Jesus said that if you are not my children, you are the children of the world. God gave us all authority to rule and reign. He allows us to put in power who we want. We have been deceived. How dare we take the coward's way out and say it is God's plan! God has a plan for redemption through the blood of Christ for us to be restored back to him. God is not mocked. Read **1 John 2:13-29**. Hitler was a type of anti-Christ. Do you believe God put him in power to do a holocaust mass murder to the apple of God's eye? We, the people, put Hitler in. We people, humans, allow that spirit in him to deceive us. There is nothing new under the sun (**Ecclesiastes 1:9**).

God allowed the Jews to be taken by Babylon because of their rebellion. He "let" does not mean that is what He wanted. That was the consequence of rebellion. He allows us to make our choices. We have His Word. Murder is sin.

Remember, you cannot serve two masters.

Church, we are doing it, doing it in the name of love. I know Martin Luther King would not have voted for color. He was a man of righteousness. He would have voted for righteousness. This spirit of anti-Christ is in the church as well as in the world.

"Beloved, believe not every spirit, but try the spirits whether they are of God: because many false prophets are gone out into the world. Hereby know ye the Spirit of God: Every spirit that confesseth that Jesus Christ is come in the flesh is of God: And every spirit that confesseth not that Jesus Christ is come in the flesh is not of God: and this is that spirit of antichrist, whereof ye have heard that it should come; and even now already is it in the world. Ye are of God, little children, and have overcome them: because greater is he that is in you, than he that is in the world. They are of the world: therefore speak they of the world, and the world heareth them." 1 John 4:1-5

I am not "anti" any man or any leader of the world but the spirit behind their sin. They are deceived, and we know better, but we have just realized how deceived the church is that so many voted the way of the anti-Christ spirit. Paul says that in the last days many will be deceived, even the elect **(Mark 13:22)**. The elect: the Jew, the Christian. Then the church goes in the name of God and prays to cover the anti-Bible and the anti-Christ spirit. What's the difference? Satan will be the final anti-Christ. Will we bless him as well? We have compromised the church, the word, and God's people. The United Nations is the anti-Christ system, the world. The devil has been working on this

163

since the beginning, but we have the spirit of truth. Many of our brothers have been seduced and compromised and have become weak just like Sampson. This is why the church is in such a powerless state, but I believe we are growing our hair back. There will be one last eruption of power. We must wake up. Black or white: Back to the Word. Then we say, "Well, God let it happen. If God didn't want it, he would have lost the election." Wrong. We are deceived. This spirit has false love. It loves the creation more than the creator. It hides behind global warming, lab testing on animals, saving the forest. If you mess with a turtle egg, it is a felony, five years in jail. I'm not against this, but you talk to any of these radicals and ask them what they think about abortion, and they will tell you it is a woman's right. Now wild animals are more valuable than God's image bearers. The anti-Christ spirit is deceiving the world that we can walk in perfect peace and harmony. We know that will never happen until Jesus comes.

We cannot co-exist with the devil. Once he deceives our trust - Look out! Then the switch will come and anyone that does not follow him will bow down to his system, the god of this world – the anti-Christ. He will kill the remaining – the stage is set. It's time, Church, to sound the alarm. This spirit will feed the poor, clothe the naked, speak false love, make the righteous look like the evil ones, stop wars, give false hope, stand back, and have false humility. It does not stand up for righteousness. Even in the church, if we stood up for righteousness, many of our brothers would tag us as prejudiced and judgmental. Yes, I am prejudice against the anti-Christ and everything he stands for. This same spirit is taking hold of pastors and leaders in the church. That is why you are not allowed to move in the anointing and the power that God has bestowed upon us. Remember, anti is against; anointing is Christ, the anointed one and his anointing. So anything against Christ and what he stands for is anti-Christ. We always put some big monster or ruler behind it. However, from the beginning, since he fell like lightning, then deceived Eve, he is now deceiving us, the Church. They say things like, "Well, you really don't need God's power. It's scaring people. You must stand for who God put in power." No, the Bible says that every ordinance and law by rulers and governors is the law of the land, but if they cause you to sin against God, then do not obey the law.

Remember Daniel and the three Jewish boys, Shadrach, Meshach, and Abednego? Try to tell me that we are not changing the meaning of the Word and smacking title grace on it!

"Saying, Did not we straightly command you that ye should not teach in this name? and, behold, ye have filled Jerusalem with your doctrine, and intend to bring this man's blood upon us. Then Peter and the other apostles answered and said, We ought to obey God rather than men." Acts 5:28-29

Example 1: There is a law that states that men cannot walk on the right side of the street facing north. Well, that does not cause me to sin. It's dumb, but God will expect me to obey. I better.

165

Example 2: They put up a statue of a president and make a law saying that once a year you must go to this statue and pray and say it is your god. This is against God's word. That is when we do not have to obey the law of the land.

See the difference? So my prayer is that God will open up our eyes. I know that many of you know this and have not erred from the faith. So I believe this word will encourage you. If you have been deceived, just repent and stay in his word. Be careful who you allow to feed you spiritually. Remember: If we leave God's word, we leave his covering, and deception is imminent. Don't rely on a man; don't rely on a denomination; rely on Him and His word alone.

Definition of deception: the act of being deceived; fraud. Definition of deceived: 1. To mislead by false appearance or statement. 2. To be unfaithful to one (spouse or God).

Remember if you think you can't be deceived, then chances are you just might be.

"Notwithstanding I have a few things against thee, because thou sufferest that woman Jezebel, which calleth herself a prophetess, to teach and to seduce my servants to commit fornication, and to eat things sacrificed unto idols. And I gave her space to repent of her fornication; and she repented not. Behold, I will cast her into a bed, and them that commit adultery with her into great tribulation, except they repent of their deeds. And I will kill her children with death; and all the churches shall know that I am he which searcheth the reins and

hearts: and I will give unto every one of you according to your works." Revelation 2:20-23

These leaders and many rulers claim to be Christians, but the Bible talks about them as well.

"Beware of false prophets, which come to you in sheep's clothing, but inwardly they are ravening wolves." Matthew 7:15

"And many false prophets shall rise, and shall deceive many." Matthews 24:11

"For there shall arise false Christs, and false prophets, and shall shew great signs and wonders; insomuch that, if it were possible, they shall deceive the very elect." Matthew 24:24

Another truth: Here are the facts. I'm not against this precious soul: the new leader of this nation. Remember, he has many anti-Christ spirits around him - Democrats, Republicans, other political parties. Some of them are forcing issues to make this nation come against God's principles. What we see in the spirit, the unseen realm, is what the Bible says is real. This is the reality. The demonic forces and strongholds have their own government. The spirit deceiving our leader might not even be the head in the spiritual realm. Remember, our leader says he is a Christian, but Jesus said you will know my disciples by their fruits and by their deeds.

"Beware of false prophets, which come to you in sheep's clothing, but inwardly they are ravening wolves. Ye shall know them by their fruits. Do men gather grapes of thorns, or figs of thistles? Even so every good tree bringeth forth good fruit; but a corrupt tree bringeth forth evil fruit. A good tree cannot bring forth evil fruit, neither can a corrupt tree bring forth good fruit. Every tree that bringeth not forth good fruit is hewn down, and cast into the fire. 20Wherefore by their fruits ye shall know them. Not everyone that saith unto me, Lord, Lord, shall enter into the kingdom of heaven; but he that doeth the will of my Father which is in heaven." Matthew 7:15-21

"And many false prophets shall rise, and shall deceive many." Matthew 24:11

This also proves that you can sit in a church for twenty years and still never be converted because when you are converted, your values change and Christ becomes your focus.

"Therefore if any man be in Christ, he is a new creature: old things are passed away; behold, all things are become new. You must be born again to enter into the kingdom of heaven."
2 Corinthians 5:17

The Greek translated as born again is born from above - no longer you, but Christ being formed in you. Most of us know this, but there are churches that have seduced entire congregations to vote against righteousness for their own satisfaction, erring from the faith. This is

168

deception. The enemy of God - the prince of this world - has been planning and setting all this up for years. There is no going back to the way things were. These places have been deceived, not letting gifts and anointing be released (religion), having cultural bias, meaning my creed, color, or ethnic makeup, putting it before His Word, and being deceived by the newspaper, television, worldly news, watching the wrong things. The television influence has been working on a generation for years, putting false love before a righteous God. For example, people think: "God loves people so I know he wants this war stopped. God is love so just on this issue, I'm voting this way. I know this must be right," but there is a much, much bigger picture. This is the kingdom of light against the kingdom of darkness.

"I am come to send fire on the earth; and what will I, if it be already kindled? But I have a baptism to be baptized with; and how am I straitened till it be accomplished! Suppose ye that I am come to give peace on earth? I tell you, Nay; but rather division: For from henceforth there shall be five in one house divided, three against two, and two against three. The father shall be divided against the son, and the son against the father; the mother against the daughter, and the daughter against the mother; the mother in law against her daughter in law, and the daughter in law against her mother in law."

Luke 12:49-53

H.O.T. CHAPTER
19

PRESENT DAY TRUTH: MANNA FROM HEAVEN

My brothers and sisters, we have to preach the Word. God is showing me a lot of things, and we need to clean up, sharpen up the Word. We must not shut down God. We must go from glory to glory – not from meeting to meeting. Friends, God will not anoint another man's message or the thoughts of man expressed in the pulpit. We need to preach the Word. God's Word should bring disruption in somebody's life. God's Word will spark such a flame of desire to change. I'm sorry, but God will not anoint anything but His Word. God's Word will bring repentance, tears and joy. His Word will not return void.

With the unction of the Holy Ghost, we will see results. You will have people persecuting you. They persecuted the King. Don't think they won't try it. Bring a sharp sword for the love of your people. Remember, as good as our intentions are, only God's Word has the potential to transform a life because He alone anoints His Word. His Words will not hit the ground. It will accomplish what it is sent to do. If you are a mouth piece of God, and you are constantly saying that everything is okay, and you keep saying peace, peace, when there is none, the word in **Jeremiah 23** has a warning for you. God says those who do not bring the pure word of God to save the people are wicked. **He says in verses 23-30: "Am I a God at hand, saith the LORD, and not a God afar off? Can any hide himself in secret places that I shall not see him? saith the LORD. Do not I fill heaven and earth? saith the LORD. I have heard what the prophets said, that prophesy lies in my name, saying, I have dreamed, I have dreamed. How long shall this be in the heart of the prophets that prophesy lies? Yea, they are prophets of the deceit of their own heart; Which think to cause my people to forget my name by their dreams which they tell every man to his neighbor, as their fathers have forgotten my name for Baal. The prophet that hath a dream, let him tell a dream; and he that hath my word, let him speak my word faithfully. What is the chaff to the wheat? saith the LORD. Is not my word like as a fire? saith the LORD; and like a hammer that breaketh the rock in pieces? Therefore, behold, I am against the prophets, saith the LORD, that steal my words everyone from his neighbor."**

We must turn sinners from their sins. We have to be careful not to cover the iniquity with grace, grace, grace. We cannot tickle the ears of God's people. We cannot tell them that they are okay. God says the wages of sin is death. God always has something you must do before his love and grace can fall on someone. Example: "When my people who are called by my name, humble themselves, cry out, turn from their wicked ways. Then I will heal their land." See? Right here, three things God says before he will forgive: turn, humble, cry out.

Please hear my heart. I love God's people. God says that there are men who have perverted the word of the living God. Listen, Church, God says that he who preaches like this, he will forget you and your city, and he will cast you out of his presence. God says, "Spare the rod, spoil the child. Train a child in the way to go and he will not depart from it. My children perish for lack of knowledge." Because I'm being obedient to God, I know He is saying, "Well done. You always told them the truth. Son, I'm so pleased with you." That should be the cry of your heart. Please God rather than man. Church, when God starts to move in a church, reverence it. Don't quench the Holy Spirit. God says, "As a dog goes back to its vomit, so a man goes back to his folly." The fear of the Lord is the beginning of wisdom. Don't let the people be left open to seducing spirits.

"The Spirit speaks, expressing in the last days that some shall depart from the faith, giving heed to seducing spirits and doctrines of devils, speaking lies and hypocrisy, having their consciences seared with a hot iron." 1 Timothy 4:1-2

This is man's words – messages that tell people how to become a better you. We need to tell them to die to themselves. Put away idols. Avoid TV until you don't watch it at all. Jezebel is flowing out of that polluted New Age box. Be careful about what goes into your eye gates. The enemy preaches his kingdom on every secular station.

Now people are getting more excited about something on television than about the Almighty God. This is what we need to preach. Live holy, die to self. What greater love does one have than to lay down his life for his brother? Our words say we love, but our words are cheap. Show me, God says. Someone could come and condemn God's people out of all their money, and nobody says anything. But try to get them to repent and give their entire lives and all they have for Christ and the Gospel, then you will see the persecution. They will not like it because, once again, it takes man out of the middle. When man has nothing to gain but God, then the tables turn! God is revealing the harlot prostitute of the church. Philosophy of men: Dirty wells that prophesy what you want to hear, not what you need. The scripture says, "Thou shall not muzzle the ox that treads out the corn. A laborer is worthy of His reward."

"Them that sin rebuke before all so that others may also fear. I charge you before God and Jesus Christ and the elect angels that you observe these without preferring one over the other, doing nothing by partiality." 1 Timothy 5:20-21

I encourage you to walk in the fear of the Lord with trembling. Pray for your brothers and sisters. The enemy has crept into the church. Pray, pray, pray. All who live godly in Christ Jesus shall suffer persecution. Evil men and seducers shall fare worse and worse, deceiving and being deceived. Continue in the thing that you have heard and learned, that have been assured by the Holy Ghost and Me.

2 Timothy 4:2 says, "Preach the word." Not a theory, not a novel. **"Be instant in season and out of**

173

season. Reprove, rebuke and exhort with all longsuffering and doctrine." We need to know that we have not yet made it into glory. There is work to do. We must smash the statues in the house of Dagon. Do not give heed to tables and commandments of men who turn from the truth. **Titus 1:9-13** says, **"Holding fast the faithful word as you have been taught that you may be able by sound doctrine both to exhort and convince the gainsayers. For there are many unruly and vain talkers and deceivers especially then of the circumcision: whose mouths must be stopped. Who subvert whole houses, teaching thing they ought not to reach for filthy lucre sake. Even a prophet of their own has said they are always liars, slow bellies, evil. This witness is true. Rebuke them sharply that they may be sound in the faith."**

Pray, Church, and go to those who oppose themselves that God peradventure will give them repentance to the knowledge of the truth that they may recover themselves out of the snare of the devil that has taken them captive at his will. The harlot of the church will die but not until the son of perdition is revealed. She is a whore of righteousness. She is after the church. Don't drink her venom. Be careful what you eat and drink at this fornicator's table. Anoint your eyes with eye salve so you may see. It is better not to eat at all than to eat this harlot's poison. Pray that I have meekness as God sends us to those who oppose themselves. God has sent many to confirm His words, and He always will. The Word says, "Let every word be established by two or three witnesses (**2 Cor 13:1**)." Even one man spoke that the Lord told him that I, Shane, was a Micaiah. I never heard that. **1 King 22:7, 8, 14** talks about Micaiah.

There were 400 prophets of the King. Jehoshaphat asked, **"Is there not a prophet of the LORD here whom we can inquire of?"** The king of Israel answered Jehoshaphat, **"There is still one man through whom we can inquire of the LORD, but I hate him because he never prophesies anything good about me, but always bad. He is Micaiah son of Imlah."**

The king called for him and he went and spoke the truth. All the other prophets spoke well of the king with one mouth, the congregation. Then Micaiah said, **"As the Lord lives what the lord says to me, that is what I will speak."** That's my covenant with my God. I bless you brother for that confirmation, and I bless every brother and sister that was obedient to speak to me to keep me in line so the devil could not twist my words and put me in a pit. It goes on to say, "The Lord put a lying spirit on all the other prophets." You don't have to look far for a prophet, a preacher or a leader in these last days who will tell you what you want to hear for sure. This prophet would rather say good things always instead of saying that which would save the church and the children of God. Some of these prophets know that if they say everything, they may not be allowed back for an offering - these prophets travel with lying spirits that actually come to houses and impart these seducing spirits in the place where the door is open. They don't even realize the damage that the devil is doing to the body. Through

175

them, the gifts are without repentance. Brother and sister, you better test the spirit, even if it is somebody you respect or the pastor says he is a true prophet. You never know when and where that well has been polluted - for the gifts of God have been prostituted in the house of God, instructing prophets to speak to certain people, one preferred over the other. Prophecy is okay, prophesy one to another to edify the body, but if you are called to the office of a prophet, don't ever prophesy to anyone unless the Lord has instructed you to.

Well, I want to thank you, precious saints. We love you. We thank God for fresh manna from the throne of God. I encourage you to walk in the fear of the Lord. Turn off your television. If it is too much temptation, get rid of it. Protect the gates of your soul. Remember: Jesus loves you, and so do we.

"See that you do not refuse him that speaks. For if they escaped not, who refused him that spoke on earth, much more shall we not escape, for if we turn away him that speaks from heaven and this word, yet once more signify the removing of those things that are shaken as of the things that are made that those things that cannot be shaken remain."

Hebrews 12:25-29

Wherefore we receive a Kingdom which cannot be moved, let us have grace, whereby we may serve God acceptably with reverence and Godly fear. For our God is a consuming fire.

"The ear that hears the reproof of life abides among the wise. He that refuses instruction despises his own soul; but he that hears reproof get understanding. The fear of the Lord is the instruction of wisdom and before honor is humility."

Proverbs 15:31-33

"He that covers his sins shall not prosper but whosoever confesses and forsake them shall have mercy. Happy is the man that fears always but he that harden his heart shall fall into mischief." Proverbs 28:13-14

"Nevertheless, I have this against you: You tolerate that woman Jezebel, who calls herself a prophetess. By her teaching she seduces my servants into sexual immorality and the eating of food sacrificed to idols. I have given her time to repent of her immorality, but she is unwilling. So I will cast her on a bed of suffering, and I will make those who commit adultery with her suffer intensely, unless they repent of her ways. I will strike her children dead. Then all the churches will know that I am he who searches hearts and minds, and I will repay each of you according to your deeds. Now I say to the rest of you in Thyatira *(in the church)*, to you who do not have this doctrine have not learned Satan's so-called deep secrets *(I will not impose any other burden on you:* Only hold on to what you have until I come. To him who overcomes and does my will to the end, I will give authority over the nations— He will rule them with a rod of iron; he will dash them to pieces like pottery'— just as I have received authority from my Father. I will also give him the morning star. He, who has an ear, let him hear what the Spirit says to the churches." Revelation 2:20-29

177

{ DO YOU HEAR THE COCK CROWING? }

We see in this modern day westernized world a gospel illusion. What you see is not what it is. Many of you are following another spirit, another gospel, another Jesus. Jesus said blessed are those who are persecuted. Peter denied Jesus three times, but once he got the Holy Ghost, he never again denied him. Many Holy Ghost claimers deny Jesus constantly. See. There are many false brethren.

"But rejoice, inasmuch as ye are partakers of Christ's sufferings; that, when his glory shall be revealed, ye may be glad also with exceeding joy." 1 Peter 4:13

"And if children, then heirs; heirs of God, and joint-heirs with Christ; if so be that we suffer with him, that we may be also glorified together." Romans 8:17 We are the Body of Christ. Christ cannot deny Himself!

"If we suffer, we shall also reign with him: if we deny him, he also will deny us: If we believe not, yet he abideth faithful: he cannot deny himself." 2 Timothy 2:12-13

Peter warming himself around the fire, seeking the cozy place. A fleshy comfort. All around him, there were mockers, gainsayers, and persecutors. This was the pinnacle point of Jesus' persecution.

"Then took they him, and led him, and brought him into the high priest's house. And Peter followed afar off. 55 And when

178

they had kindled a fire in the midst of the hall, and were set down together, Peter sat down among them. 56 But a certain maid beheld him as he sat by the fire, and earnestly looked upon him, and said, This man was also with him. And he denied him, saying, Woman, I know him not. And after a little while another saw him, and said, Thou art also of them. And Peter said, Man, I am not. And about the space of one hour after another confidently affirmed, saying, Of a truth this fellow also was with him: for he is a Galilaean. And Peter said, Man, I know not what thou sayest. And immediately, while he yet spake, the cock crew. And the Lord turned, and looked upon Peter. And Peter remembered the word of the Lord, how he had said unto him, Before the cock crow, thou shalt deny me thrice. And Peter went out, and wept bitterly."

Luke 22:54-62

There was not a problem with Jesus. It was Peter. Jesus was doing what he was born to do. Jesus was seeing that he was not ready to walk in this high level of ministry. Peter thought he was ready. Jesus was broken for Peter. Peter saw the mission trips of Jesus. Peter saw the salvations. Peter saw the demons tremble. He dined with Him. They broke bread. Peter had fear of being associated with this radical Truth and anointed man of God. Peter's reputation was on the line. God says your reputation will get in the way of your destination. Lose it, because it is not who you are. Who are we denying? Christ? Or are you trying to protect your reputation in perilous times? Are you scared to stand? What click are you hanging with around the fire? Are we scared to admit to being associated with Christ and His

179

sufferings? We see in this nation westernized philosophies and fairy tale gospels, false love that provokes no persecution. You, Peter – born again believer - have now the gift of the Holy Ghost. Peter was endued with power and never again denied Truth. You want power? Man up! We have brothers and sisters in this nation and the nations of the world under persecution, mostly in this nation from carnal Christians. In this nation, it is a persecution of silence. Knowing truth, still keeping quiet. Time to stand with Jesus. Be delivered from the fear of man.

America, wake up!

God is cleaning the pulpits, separating sheep from the goats. Remember, those who live Godly in Christ Jesus shall suffer persecution. Let the persecuted of the Lord find one another. Know that they hate you without a cause because they know Him not. Spirit of Truth bears witness with the truth that we are the sons of God. It's time to flee houses of untempered mortar, man's will, humanistic mixture pulpits. Paul said that He does not come in man's wisdom but in power. It's time to stop being Jezebel's eunuchs and become bold, righteous lions. God is showing the house to the House. Can you hear what the Spirit is saying to the Church?

HOLINESS

Compromise, oh, how you compromise my ways for your ways! I am against those preachers who preach peace when there is no peace. They have seduced my people with seductive words and flattering divinations. They talk about the things of this world. They boast on things they should not.

"For there shall be no more any vain vision nor flattering divination within the house of Israel. For I *am* the LORD: I will speak, and the word that I shall speak shall come to pass; it shall be no more prolonged: for in your days, O rebellious house, will I say the word, and will perform it, saith the Lord GOD." Ezekiel 12:24-25

"Son of man, behold, *they of* the house of Israel say, The vision that he seeth *is* for many days *to come*, and he prophesieth of the times *that are* far off." Ezekiel 12:27

Now is that far off time. Church, you have been inked and flattered by saying prophets have passed away. We have a gift to edify one another. Don't you know Paul was prophet, James was prophet? The office of a prophet is totally different. Have I not said I will send the spirit of Elijah in the last days? These prophets will tear down the fornicators in my house.

"**Therefore say unto them, Thus saith the Lord GOD; There shall none of my words be prolonged any more, but the word which I have spoken shall be done, saith the Lord GOD.**" Ezekiel 12:28

Read **Chapter 13 and 14 of Ezekiel** that says, "Prophesy against the prophets, the preachers..." It talks about the stiff-necked rebellious children, those prophets and preachers who speak out of their own heart, says the Lord.

[Note: The following passage is a combination of scripture and prophetic utterance as given to the author by the Lord.]

I have the word of the Lord: " Woe unto the foolish preachers and prophets that follow their own spirit and have seen nothing. O church, they are like foxes in the deserts. They have seen vanity, lying divinations, says the Lord. I have not sent them. They have made others to hope that they would confirm the Word. They are like foxes without holes. They scurry around day to day and week to week trying to come up with new ideas on how to build their own kingdoms. They are houses built with straw. My hand shall be on the preacher and prophets that speak vanity and divine lies. Behold, I am against them. They shall surely be cut out of the assembly of my people because they have seduced my people, saying peace when there is no peace. One built up a wall and the other helped to build with untendered mortar. Say to them that work for the man that they shall surely fall and turn to dust. Shall not the earth swallow up every manmade Kingdom and ministry that I have not built? The stormy wind shall rend it. When it has fallen, woe unto those who shall fall to dust with that house. There shall be an overflowing shower of my anger and great hailstones of my fury. I will break down the walls that have been built by the hands of man. They say this is done in the name of the Lord. The foundation of that house shall be discovered. Those prophets and preachers make idols in their hearts.

They rend to Caesar but not to the Almighty. Their television set is their God. Their building is their God. Have I not said, You shall have no other gods before me? Yet you betray me with a kiss every day. You build monuments in my name, statues in my name. You pervert the way of the righteous. I shall break every idol to pieces. Woe unto the woman who sew pillows to all armholes and make handkerchiefs upon your heads. Upon statures to hunt souls! Will you hunt the souls of my people, will you save the souls alive that come to you? Will you pollute my people for a little grain and barley, for bread? You have made the heart of the righteous sad with lies. I shall deliver my people out of the hand of vain prophets and preachers. To the elder in my house who have set up idols in these hearts and put a stumbling block of their iniquity before

183

their face, I say to every man of the house of God that sets up idols in his heart and puts a stumbling block of their iniquity before their face and comes to the prophet: I, the Lord, will answer Him according to the multitude of his idols. They are all estranged from me with their idols. Repent and turn yourselves from your idols. Turn your faces from your abominations all who separate themselves from me and set up idols in your hearts. I will set my face against that man and cut him off from the midst of my people. If a prophet be deceived when He has spoken a thing, I the Lord will deceive that prophet. I will put my hand upon him, and I will destroy him out of the midst of my people. The punishment of that prophet or preacher shall be great and him that chase shall be great and him that chase that prophet shall be punished also.

Please test every prophecy. Be not deceived when someone says God is here, and you don't see Him. Don't think you are missing Him. He's not there. For the vain and arrogant of my house, those men and woman who have led my sheep away, who have scattered the righteous, shall I not punish the watchman that I have assigned who have brought these in? Heresies. You who team up on the righteous, who find fault in my remnant? You don't fear your thoughts. You have secretly spoken, but I have heard you.

Plot your mischief. You forsake my anointed. You do not fear me. You think I am afar off."

"I will therefore put you in remembrance, though ye once knew this, how that the Lord, having saved the people out of the land of Egypt, afterward destroyed them that believed not. And the angels which kept not their first estate, but left their own habitation, he hath reserved in everlasting chains under darkness unto the judgment of the great day. Even as Sodom and Gomorrah, and the cities about them in like manner, giving themselves over to fornication, and going after strange flesh, are set forth for an example, suffering the vengeance of eternal fire. Likewise these *filthy* dreamers defile the flesh, despise dominion, and speak evil of dignities. Yet Michael the archangel, when contending with the devil he disputed about the body of Moses, durst not bring against him a railing accusation, but said, The Lord rebuke thee. But these speak evil of those things which they know not: but what they know naturally, as brute beasts, in those things they corrupt themselves. Woe unto them! for they have gone in the way of Cain, and ran greedily after the error of Balaam for reward, and perished in the gainsaying of Core. These are spots in your feasts of charity, when they feast with you, feeding themselves without fear: clouds *they are* without water, carried about of winds; trees whose fruit withereth, without fruit, twice dead, plucked up by the roots." Jude 1:5-12

I tell you that if this word of God does not put the fear of the Lord in you, then you don't believe His word or His prophets. May we all fear and walk in the way of righteousness, putting aside everything that hinders love in our hearts.

21

SPIRIT & TRUTH

The word of the Lord: **"This is the time. I'm opening up revelation, Insight, and kingdom."**

I was in a meeting in a local church where a very well-known prophet was visiting. I'm glad I went. I got a good word of confirmation and direction and knowledge from heaven. In this meeting, the Spirit was really strong. His presence was just like it is here (at H.O.T. House of Truth). I was very happy to feel and see that many are drinking up living water. Then I returned home and went to sleep.

I had a dream. In this dream there was this pastor. He had big, I mean, the biggest pens with his church name on it. Let me share this first: Many people are trying to copy this great pastor in California. This church is great but still lacking the fullness of the apostolic church. Many have gone overboard with this very known leader. They idolize him. This is not all his fault, but we have to stop man worship. Honor and idolatry are totally different. We must love and present the truth. Many pastors are hiring people to grow their churches. God has His way. It is called glory! These pastors want a big name, a big building, and a big crowd to follow them. Why are they getting a big crowd? Because they are holding back the Truth. There is no victory without the Truth. You can have the Spirit and not the Truth. That's the Truth, meaning that you allow the Holy Spirit to move among you and touch you.

In this meeting, I even heard the cry, "We want meat!" to this visiting prophet. The Body is starving because they want the Spirit. They want the true Word to be preached. Most people are looking for both: Spirit and Truth.

Back to the dream. These pens were huge. You know those advertisement pens. Well, they shrunk in the container, and this pastor got very angry and stretched them bigger. He was determined to advertize the most, to have the most followers and the biggest church. These are carnal motives. These are driven by the flesh of men. We are not to be relevant with the world. We are a peculiar people. A royal people. We are light. We want to entertain people instead of directing them from sin. God is going to purify His bride. We are already clean by His blood, but His plan is not for us to live in bondage to anything that the world has to offer. Jesus was not at all like them – the World. They thought He was like them, but they were wrong because one problem is that these pastors aren't supposed to lead the people. They are nurturers. They change diapers and pick up the kids when they fall. They bring the family of God to revelation, but they are not apostles or prophets. The devil has made the pastoral church, and it is out of order. This is the year of authority and government. Praise God that some of these pastors are apostles, but because of false order, they carry the load. Most are not apostles and because of that the Body has not been able to grow up normally. They have been so used to being pampered and being babies that when a prophet or an apostle comes to them with the Truth, they run because they have lived in a fatherless, out of order church. If you offer your kids candy and pudding, cupcakes, and sweet words all the time, and someone comes along and says, "Hey, here is some spinach, carrots, and filet mignon," what will their reaction be? Kids hate vegetables and have not yet acquired a taste for filet mignon. Where do you think all the baby spirit born kids will flock?

Spirit and Truth together: the only balanced diet! Not one is better than the other.

So in my dream, I was now in a classroom. The desks were all messed up. There was a projector cart, and on it was a big, I mean huge, rice crispy marshmallow puff. I walked over and took what they were serving and began to eat. "It is so good.." Then I said "No," and I stopped eating

188

it. When I eat a lot of carbs and sugar, I gain weight. It is not good for me. Then I said, "This will kill me." Although I wanted to eat more, I stopped myself and said no. Then I looked over, and there were Marlboro cigarette packs stacked on some of the desks, letting me know that many are in bondage because they are not being preached the truth. Grace, grace is all that they put in their faces. Jesus said you shall know the Truth and the Truth will set you free.

Everything is good. Everything is sweet. Not ever knowing that they are shackled at their feet. That it is out of order means just that: It is out of order.

"That we henceforth be no more children, tossed to and fro, and carried about with every wind of doctrine, by the sleight of men, and cunning craftiness, whereby they lie in wait to deceive; But speaking the truth in love, may grow up into him in all things, which is the head, even Christ: From whom the whole body fitly joined together and compacted by that which every joint supplieth, according to the effectual working in the measure of every part, maketh increase of the body unto the edifying of itself in love." Ephesians 4:14-16

Pastors, find your place. God is setting things in order, and when His truth comes, you will and are being exposed. Control and manipulation will be exposed. It is time that the Body of Christ grows into maturity, and you need to let the Truth come in. You have people worshipping in Spirit but not in Truth.

"But the hour cometh, and now is, when the true worshippers shall worship the Father in spirit and in truth: for the Father

189

seeketh such to worship him. **God is a Spirit: and they that worship him must worship him in spirit and in truth. The woman saith unto him, I know that Messias cometh, which is called Christ: when he is come, he will tell us all things."**

John 4:23-25

Get your fantasy church out of your mind. Let God's government come in so that the power and transformation can come. You will be exposed by the Truth. Your gift makes room for you. Only the Truth sets people free.

"Then said Jesus to those Jews which believed on him, If ye continue in my word, then are ye my disciples indeed; And ye shall know the truth, and the truth shall make you free. They answered him, We be Abraham's seed, and were never in bondage to any man: how sayest thou, Ye shall be made free? Jesus answered them, Verily, verily, I say unto you, Whosoever committeth sin is the servant of sin. And the servant abideth not in the house for ever: but the Son abideth ever. If the Son therefore shall make you free, ye shall be free indeed." John 8:31-36

You see, this will stop all baby stuff, and we will enjoy Him and His presence the way we are supposed to mature, not acting like little kids but like warriors, lovers of God. But not leaving the innocence of coming to Him as a little child, believing, trusting, and moving in Him. Jesus wasn't trying to please the crowd.

"Then went the Pharisees, and took counsel how they might entangle him in his talk. And they sent out unto him their

190

disciples with the Herodians, saying, Master, we know that thou art true, and teachest the way of God in truth, neither carest thou for any man: for thou regardest not the person of men." Matthew 22:15-16

Isn't this great? God is bringing back righteousness and the Spirit. He is so good. Don't think that the enemy cannot come in the midst of the presence of God. Remember: Peter was influenced by Satan, Judas was overtaken by the enemy, and they walked with Him, the living Word.

God allowed Judas to kill himself because he was in bondage to religion, jealousy, and strife. He would have contaminated the new church from the start. They didn't even know what Judas was up to, but Jesus did, and now we can also because we have the Truth inside of us.

The real Jesus is arising in His church, and He is offensive, and He is bold, and He is love.

"Unto you therefore which believe he is precious: but unto them which be disobedient, the stone which the builders disallowed, the same is made the head of the corner, And a stone of stumbling, and a rock of offence, even to them which stumble at the word, being disobedient: whereunto also they were appointed. But ye are a chosen generation, a royal priesthood, an holy nation, a peculiar people; that ye should shew forth the praises of him who hath called you out of darkness into his marvelous light." 1 Peter 2:7-9

He is setting His house back in order. Pastors will have to line up or they will miss what they have been looking for. Jesus pronounced judgment on sin. He had authority wherever He went, but He did not force His authority. He leads in meekness and humbleness. Where He was not accepted, He left. God is raising up true, apostolic fathers. You have felt the shift. You will see the fruit. False apostles will be found lying. You will know them by their fruit not their titles. It's all good, but it's hard to change. Truth will come and will remain. What worked years ago is not going to work now. God says, "We need not to just blow up. We need to grow up." Your little fantasy will not be stronger than God's ways. He is bringing order. You cannot truly worship in Truth when you are in bondage because your heart, as much as it wants to be, is on other things. He is looking for Spirit and Truth together, for pure undefiled worship.

The ecclesia (church) is arising and is hot. Can you feel the flames of His desire for all of you? Mary worshipped in Spirit. She didn't even know who she was, yet in Him, she was moved by the Spirit. She did not even realize she was preparing His body for burial. Many of the twelve worshipped Jesus in truth but when He presented it to the crowd in John chapter 6, they didn't like the Truth. It was too much for them to bear, I mean, to pick up their cross and follow Him.

Deny yourself. After that it said in **John 6:66** that many of His disciples walked with Him no more, but the chosen stayed and worshipped and told Him that He had the Words of life after speaking the Truth! Are you bringing division with the Truth? Or are you drawing a crowd with a compromised sugar-coated gospel? Yum, yum donuts, or are you, no matter how many people hate you, bringing the Truth of the full gospel in love and not leaving the Spirit behind? This is what God is looking for. This is the new wine. Will you drink this cup? Grace and truth together are the gospel. Don't let them fool you. Righteousness is not legalism. Legalism is dry, powerless, and dead. Righteousness is bold, is powerful, and is Truth wrapped in the presence of God. Let us eat His flesh and drink His blood so that we can have power and stop chasing the baby relevant church. Take dominion, take authority, take up your cross and follow Him, not a move, not a feeling, not a man, but follow Him, Christ!

{ SPIRIT OF TRUTH AND SPIRIT OF ERROR }

A false prophet is not just someone who misses a prophetic word. A false prophet is someone who comes to you in sheep's clothing but inwardly is a ravaging wolf (**Matthew 7:15**). God says there are so many on media, internet, Facebook, YouTube.... Any messenger who doesn't speak by the Spirit of God is a false prophet and they are always led by the Spirit of Error!

They will take scripture out of context to promote themselves or their agenda. They will sooth-say, tickle your ears, and build you up in the flesh, not help you to deny yourself but actually indulge in the rudiments of the world. They will always be defending themselves because they are always in some kind of situation that needs to be reasoned out.

A true Messenger's message, led by the Spirit of Truth, will always line up with the word of God, whether it is a word of wisdom or prophecy. A false prophet - whatever proceeds out of your mouth or spirit is not from the Holy Spirit. God said that we judge whether words come from God or Satan or man. Man's wisdom vs. God's wisdom. **Colossians 2:8**. Only God knows the secrets of man's hearts. He will expose them to those who have pure motives, undefiled religion. **James 1:27**

A true prophet will protect the sheep from any wolf that comes. Arrogant, prideful, and self promoters will wax worse and worse as the anti-Christ spirit builds its church and platform.

Real prophets will get stoned to hold onto truth and will not back down. Let me tell you, there are far less true prophets in the body of Christ than are proclaimed. Most of them do not title themselves because the spirit of truth is lowly and humble.

The enemy can give an accurate word of knowledge. How? - because they are in the world and know things. So we test the words coming forth to see if they bear witness to our spirits. When the Holy Spirit is grieved in a meeting everyone feels Him leave. It is not from God. A word of wisdom is not wisdom if it contradicts God's word and does not set you apart. A false prophet can say something true, but The Spirit of God is not on it, so many are being deceived by men and women building their own platform and who haven't been set in by God. God promises to put a lying spirit in the mouth of these false prophets. It will become clearer and clearer who is speaking from the spirit of truth and from the spirit error and religion. .

"We are of God: he that knoweth God heareth us; he that is not of God heareth not us. Hereby know we the spirit of truth, and the spirit of error." 1 John 4:6

JACOB AND ESAU

"Esau I hate. Jacob I love." Two Jews, two brothers - two children of God - one with an inheritance, one a trouble maker. Yes, I know Esau represents the Jew, and Jacob, the Gentile – he got a new name and so on, but I'm sent to the church by God. We have an inheritance given to us in **Obadiah 8**: **"Shall I not in day say the Lord destroy the wise men out of Edom and understanding out of the Mount Esau?"** In **Obadiah 17 and 18**, it says, **"but upon Mount Zion shall be deliverance and there shall be holiness; and the house of Jacob shall posses there their possessions. And the House of Jacob shall be a fire and the House of Joseph a flame and the House of Esau for stubble."**

Are you as a Gentile provoking jealousy to the Jew? Are you a house of fire? Are you a flame for Him? Are you a Jacob or an Esau chasing your belly? Do the things of God work around your schedule, your job, and your fleshly desires? Are you trading in your inheritance for your flesh? Do you have a bowl of soup that you must have? Do you have a business that has taken the throne? Do you have a hobby that's slowly becoming number one? Has God become a once or twice a week event in your life? Do not think, my brother, that you have made it yet. Work out your own salvation with fear and trembling.

God is bringing down the sword. Yet you compromise. What you think is okay, God says it is not. You say, "Oh, He is such a loving God, He will understand." You are being deceived.

Jesus Christ himself said that if you do not forsake father, mother, brother or sister, you are not worthy of me. When did Jesus change? Never.

Paul clearly said that in the last days, seducing spirits through compromising leaders and preachers have resurrected their own doctrines of devils. Everyone believes that we are in the last days, but we only take what Paul says when it is good for us. We make our own little bibles in our own minds. Some people actually write them out and have made a religion.

"But there were false prophets also among the people, even as there shall be false teachers among you, who privily shall bring in damnable heresies, even denying the Lord that bought them, and bring upon themselves swift destruction. And many shall follow their pernicious ways; by reason of whom the way of truth shall be evil spoken of. And through covetousness shall

197

they with feigned words make merchandise of you: whose judgment now of a long time lingereth not, and their damnation slumbereth not. For if God spared not the angels that sinned, but cast *them* down to hell, and delivered *them* into chains of darkness, to be reserved unto the judgment; And spared not the old world, but saved Noah the eighth *person,* a preacher of righteousness, bringing in the flood upon the world of the ungodly; And turning the cities of Sodom and Gomorrha into ashes condemned *them* with an overthrow, making *them* an ensample unto those that after should live ungodly; And delivered just Lot, vexed with the filthy conversation of the wicked: (For that righteous man dwelling among them, in seeing and hearing, vexed *his* righteous soul from day to day with *their* unlawful deeds;)The Lord knoweth how to deliver the godly out of temptations, and to reserve the unjust unto the day of judgment to be punished: But chiefly them that walk after the flesh in the lust of uncleanness, and despise government. Presumptuous *are they,* self-willed, they are not afraid to speak evil of dignities." 2 Peter 2:1-10

"Who verily was foreordained before the foundation of the world, but was manifest in these last times for you, Who by him do believe in God, that raised him up from the dead, and gave him glory; that your faith and hope might be in God."

1 Peter 1:20-21

People in the church are writing compromising books, *"How to Get Rich Quick,"* books with biblical

198

principles by doctor so and so. Church, Jesus said in **Revelation 2:24-29, "But unto you I say and to the rest in the church as many as have not this doctrine and have not known the depths of Satan as they speak I will put on you no other burden but that which you have hold fast till I come and He that overcome and keep my Word until the end – to him I'll give power over the nations and he shall rule them with a rood of iron; as the vessels of a potter shall they be broken to shivers; even as I received of my Father. And I will give him the morning star. He that has an ear let him hear what the spirit says unto the churches."**

Jesus said in **Revelation 3:16, "because you are lukewarm neither hot nor cold I will spew you out of my mouth."** He is saying that because of the nice things you have, you are comfortable. You say: "My bills are paid." "I got a good job." "I go to church. I even tithe." "Sometimes, I help around the church." Don't you know that God says that you are miserable, poor, blind and naked? In verses 18 and 19, He is saying, **"I counsel you to buy gold tried in the fire that you may be rich and that the shame of your nakedness does not appear. Anoint your eyes with eye salve that you may see. As many as I love I rebuke and chasten. Be zealous and repent."**

So we need to repent as many times as we are convicted. By His word in **Matthew 24:13, "But he that**

endures until the end him shall be saved." Remember, just because you called on the name of Jesus one day doesn't mean that you got a free ticket to glory. Don't you know it is the goodness of God that brings sinners to repent, but it is the word untouched, unchanged, the Word of God that keeps a man in a life of repentance? Those who endure to the end shall be saved. The Word will keep you!

"Thus saith the LORD of hosts, Hearken not unto the words of the prophets that prophesy unto you: they make you vain: they speak a vision of their own heart, *and* not out of the mouth of the LORD. They say still unto them that despise me, The LORD hath said, Ye shall have peace; and they say unto every one that walketh after the imagination of his own heart, No evil shall come upon you. For who hath stood in the counsel of the LORD, and hath perceived and heard his word? who hath marked his word, and heard *it?* Behold, a whirlwind of the LORD is gone forth in fury, even a grievous whirlwind: it shall fall grievously upon the head of the wicked. The anger of the LORD shall not return, until he have executed, and till he have performed the thoughts of his heart: in the latter days ye shall consider it perfectly. I have not sent these prophets, yet they ran: I have not spoken to them, yet they prophesied. But if they had stood in my counsel, and had caused my people to hear my words, then they should have turned them from their evil way, and from the evil of their doings. *Am* I a God at hand, saith the LORD, and not a God afar off? Can any hide himself

200

in secret places that I shall not see him? saith the LORD. Do not I fill heaven and earth? saith the LORD. I have heard what the prophets said, that prophesy lies in my name, saying, I have dreamed, I have dreamed. How long shall *this* be in the heart of the prophets that prophesy lies? yea, *they are* prophets of the deceit of their own heart; Which think to cause my people to forget my name by their dreams which they tell every man to his neighbour, as their fathers have forgotten my name for Baal. The prophet that hath a dream, let him tell a dream; and he that hath my word, let him speak my word faithfully. What *is* the chaff to the wheat? saith the LORD. *Is* not my word like as a fire? saith the LORD; and like a hammer *that* breaketh the rock in pieces? Therefore, behold, I *am* against the prophets, saith the LORD, that steal my words every one from his neighbour. Behold, I *am* against the prophets, saith the LORD, that use their tongues, and say, He saith. Behold, I *am* against them that prophesy false dreams, saith the LORD, and do tell them, and cause my people to err by their lies, and by their lightness; yet I sent them not, nor commanded them: therefore they shall not profit this people at all, saith the LORD. And when this people, or the prophet, or a priest, shall ask thee, saying, What *is* the burden of the LORD? thou shalt then say unto them, What burden? I will even forsake you, saith the LORD." Jeremiah 23:16-33

{ EXPOSING THE THIEF }

Truly stirred and awakened to the fact that many Christians just don't get it...I want you to get this: God uses prophets today (real prophets) to expose the lies. The false prophets and false apostles...false doctrines...false teachers...they have an anointing to do so. Quit with the "judge not" stuff. It's really immature and just shows that you are not yet ready to stand for God. Who are you to charge God's elect (**Romans 8:33**)? If God uses His prophets to expose works of Satan in His church, who are you to stone the messenger? God said that He will send the spirit of Elijah before the coming of the Lord. So what did Elijah do? He killed the false prophets, exposed the heart of man, restored God's sons and daughters back to him, confronted the works of darkness....

The Cross is the narrow way, few are they that find it....Is God a man that He should lie? This Spirit of Elijah is the Spirit of truth. God promises to guide us into all truth...So how is this done? - By exposing the spirit of the era or the ant-Christ Spirit. Elijah did it. Jesus did it. John the Baptist did it. Paul did it...Will you do it or are you one that actually gets in God's way...with your westernized Jesus of your own design?

Do not muzzle the ox that treads out the corn. Judge your walk. Are you on the narrow path or have you become an enemy of the cross (**Philippians 3:17-19**)? You see, there is a crowd following another Gospel. In the end, what does this mean to you? GOD NEVER CHANGES.....LORD, WE NEED YOUR FEAR!!

What does a good shepherd do when he sees a wolf coming? Does he lead the sheep to the wolf? God said that He will raise up shepherds (**Jeremiah 23:4-6**). Real leaders fight for the sheep. Don't stick up for wolves in sheep's clothing! God is saying this: Whose side are you on? If Truth be your God, serve Him. If deception is your desire, serve him, but get out of God's way. If you do not have the anointing or grace, then it is not your place. Step out. You better know what spirit is leading you!

THESE ARE SERIOUS TIMES and God is getting serious telling you now! Have you not heard of the zeal for his House? Ask God to baptize you in that (**Psalm 69:9**) (**John 2:17**)!! IT'S AWESOME!!! WAKE UP! Not everyone next to you is heading to the same place. IT'S TIME FOR THE REAL POWER OF ELIJAH TO COME FORTH. It won't look like Sunday school. AMEN! Please hear what the Spirit is saying to YOU, The Church!!!!!

ARE YOU COVERED OR SMOTHERED?

"Let no man despise your youth..." " Neglect not the gift that is in you, which was given you by prophecy..." 1 Tim 4:12,14

Can I have the truth? Every time I get some truth, some man tries to put me in a yoke. How it is that you desire to be so religious? You say, who's covering you? Isn't God big enough to cover you? Hasn't God covered the earth with His glory? The grass covers the ground. I say, "Let God's people go." You always twist the truth. Why do you always pervert the truth with your religious traditions and manipulate God's people with doctrines of your desires? You take the grace of God and turn it into works. You bring God's children back into bondage with your heresies and self-indulgence. You always keep people in the boat. My children get a "revelation," and you say, "Be careful." I see your motives. I see your schemes. I see how you think you are the one to call people into position. A little leaven leavens the whole lump. A little tradition, a little religion...you have contaminated the entire thing. Didn't Paul walk alone for three years after His conversion, teaching and preaching out of revelation? But you ask, "Who are you under? Who are you with?" I'm under the King. I would rather have a circle of friends around me baptized in the Holy Ghost because they do not have their own agendas. You say, "Well, it's time to make another deacon. Let's have a meeting. Board, who do you think we can make a deacon this week? Well, Jon Doe seems to be getting a little weary and agitated. We better make him a deacon. We don't want to lose him. All in favor say, 'Yes.'" One day I was in this place. There was a man who called himself an apostle. His goal was to see how many people or ministries he could have under his belt so he could stand up and proudly say, "I have twelve ministries under me. So listen to me." I visited once in awhile in times past. I went back to that place. I felt very out of place because everyone was ordained as an apostle. I was looking around and said to myself, "Where are they going?" They are always there. They all have churches or are under another apostle. I prefer to let others call me what they want to call me. I prefer to let God call me the way He did. Remember Paul and the other twelve - they had a meeting. It was the eleven after Judas hung himself. "I vote on Matthias. All in favor..." Hmm, I never heard another thing about him again. Oh, but Paul was God's replacement. He was never received by the others for three years. He walked with God by himself. He brought people around him, not under him. Timothy, do not despise your youth...Go, go, go. Do the works of an evangelist. Imagine, Paul says, "Timothy, I see you are a prophet. Be careful, Timothy. Follow me for twenty years, and I will meet with the other leaders in the region. Possibly we will send you then. We will give you a beautiful plaque and a golden sealed certificate.

I, Apostle Paul, will sign it." How quickly were the seventy ordained in the book of Acts? Was it after ten years of Bible School? The Master had a ministry of only three and a half years. You do the math. You let the Holy Spirit show you. Get out and away from the leaders and controlling manipulators. Walk in boldness. Submit one to another. Don't worry. They said Paul was out of order. They said Jesus was a heretic. They said God was a heretic. If we believe that Christ was God in the flesh, who is really the heretic? Get out of the boat. Quit giving all your money to a man or woman who claims to have a vision. Their only vision is to live off the sheep, to pay for their family, their car, their house and their vacation. Don't get me wrong. Pay your tithes. Give, give, give. Not to fruitless works, but to truth and to God, not to man. You'll never see a return if you give your money to a man. These leaders sit all day in their office thinking of ways to enlarge their congregation. Their building fund becomes their idol. They spend lots of money on advertising their church. Everyone in their own eyes is the best. If God does show up, it is because He promised to inhabit the praises of His people. But they call it revival. Grow up, Church. Where are the warriors? Where are the laid down lovers of God? The more I grow in Him, the more I cannot stand to be around such nonsense, but I will never give up on God's church. I will continue to love and tell the truth. That is true love, not to sugarcoat things. I use the word revival also because it is familiar, but it is not in the Bible. It is called REPENTANCE and turning back to God. The spirit of Elijah turns the hearts of the children back to the Father. That's what revival is. Repentance has become a bad word in the church. If there is the same man up front every week, that's what is out of order. You really think these people want to hear you every week? That's pride. The pulpit is God's, not yours. Your job is to push people to a higher place than you are. That's the Kingdom; not lording over them. You cry out, "God, where are the people?" God says, "As soon as you operate the way I have instructed you, the people will come." It's a new day, a new season. It is not a one man show. Everyone has a piece of the puzzle, but you would rather muzzle. Repent, leaders who have held God's people down, making them feel so bound in their gifts and calling. You are the one holding the Kingdom back. You are the one who is out of order. You say there is freedom in this place just because you let people run around the room and pray in tongues, but how much freedom is there if God tells one of your members that He does not want you, Pastor, to say anything and instructs you to sit down, and someone else takes the microphone to bring a message from the Holy Ghost even though you have worked all week on it? That is real freedom. Would you sit down? You say you would, but you are a liar because God is doing that all the time and you continue to quench the Holy Spirit, making the people fear you with your control and your manipulation. But you, the remnant, the few, the fearless, the faithful, your voice will be heard once again! God bless you, Children of God. We bless you, who are part of the few. We love you, and may the grace of God abound more and more abundantly in your lives.

CIRCUMCISING HIS BRIDE

To the bride, His beloved, His lover, the severing process is at hand. God is warning His bride. Sound the alarm. God is tearing His bride apart from the world and its demonic influences.

"And if your right hand causes you to sin, cut it off and cast it from you; for it is more profitable for you that one of your members perish, than for your whole body to be cast into hell." Matthew 5:30

"And begins to beat his fellow servants, and to eat and drink with the drunkards, the master of that servant will come on a day when he is not looking for him and at an hour that he is not aware of, and will cut him in two and appoint him his portion with the hypocrites. There shall be weeping and gnashing of teeth." Matthew 24:49-51

We must become angry by what is happening in the church as well as in the world. I repeat: Every kingdom built and run by the hands of man and the wisdom of the dollar bill will fall, and great will be that fall, and also every polluted, filthy lucre ministry will fall. You cannot serve two masters.

"And I say to you, make friends for yourselves by unrighteous mammon, that when you fail, they may receive you into an everlasting home. He who is faithful in what is least is faithful also in much; and he who is unjust in what is least is unjust also in much. Therefore if you have not been faithful in the unrighteous mammon, who will commit to your trust the true riches? And if you have not been faithful in what is another man's, who will give you what is your own? No servant can serve two masters; for either he will hate the one and love the other, or else he will be loyal to the one and despise the other. You cannot serve God and mammon." Luke 16:9-13

There is a remnant that has not bowed their knee to Baal. There is a remnant that despises sin, a bride that has not been in fornication with Delilah. Remember: The only way a husband can put away his wife is if she commits adultery. God is our husband, and we are his bride. God's law is Himself. Remember: Jesus came not to abolish but to fulfill the law. "My bride, you are sleeping with Jezebel and Delilah during the week, and then you come to romance Me on Sundays."

"And if a woman divorces her husband and marries another, she commits adultery." Mark 10:12

We are a bride; not a harlot. You do not listen to the prophets that God sends you. You call his messengers the enemy and dance all night with Jezebel. You carve pumpkins at Halloween; you hide Easter eggs on Resurrection Sunday;

at Christmas, you put your kids on Santa's lap at the mall. You vote how you feel instead of the way of righteousness. Your agenda is to be liked rather than to be persecuted. American idol has become yours, also. You have become desensitized to the Holy Spirit. On one hand, we have the legalist, like little bible Hitler's, not allowing the gifts of the spirit to operate nor the freedom and liberty, turning it into works, saying we must do something to receive from God. Then they have you. You are just like the world: You smell like them, talk like them. You are under seduction by seducing spirits. Paul clearly was warning the body about this day by saying that even the elect will be deceived. This is that day, as in the days of Noah, so are we, Church.

"Do not love the world or the things in the world. If anyone loves the world, the love of the Father is not in him."

1 John 2:15

"But now I have written to you not to keep company with anyone named a brother, who is sexually immoral, or covetous, or an idolater, or a reviler, or a drunkard, or an extortioner— not even to eat with such a person. For what have I to do with judging those also who are outside? Do you not judge those who are inside? But those who are outside God judges. Therefore "put away from yourselves the evil person."

1 Corinthians 5:11-13

Our job is not to be liked. Our job is to love. We have mixed that up, thinking we must be liked to be able to love. God is circumcising his bride at this time, cutting away the chaff. He is separating the tare from the wheat. The enemy has a plan, and so do I, says God. The news has a vein of the anti-Christ spirit. Don't listen to the world. If you do, you are listening to Satan's false prophets. Hear My true prophets and My voice.

"You are of God, little children, and have overcome them, because He who is in you is greater than he who is in the world. They are of the world. Therefore they speak as of the world, and the world hears them. We are of God. He who knows God hears us; he who is not of God does not hear us. By this we know the spirit of truth and the spirit of error."

1 John 4:4-6

The world's agenda is to make the righteous look like the enemy. Why, Church, are we doing the same?

We must wake up. Look at what must change - your thinking. If you are living against any of His word and enjoying it, means that you are living in compromise. Sampson lived like that. He was a chosen vessel. The enemy finally deceived Him and took him captive. Shake off the religious dust. Separate yourselves from the world. Be in the world but not of the world, doing, acting, thinking like them. God is not mocked. If you sow corruption or yoke up with them that do, you will reap corruption in these last days. Stay away from these world marketing schemes. The devil is trying to make every one scramble, making them focus on money instead of souls. Start your own endeavors. You are the head and not the tail. Put your hand to the plow and advance God's kingdom and not your own!

"Beware lest anyone cheat you through philosophy and empty deceit, according to the tradition of men, according to the basic principles of the world, and not according to Christ." Colossians 2:8

Do not be unequally yoked with unbelievers. Support His kingdom. "I am allowing the mighty dollar to lose its power. Then you will return to me. I am almighty. The banking system of this world will fail you, will rob you. I have My system in place. You are granted a return in this time as well as in heaven. Don't put your trust in earth, but put it back in Me." God says, "You are my warrior; come out of the enemy camp and fight for Me. Quit contaminating yourselves! I have given you power over sin. I will put you away from Me, if you do not return to your first love."

"Pure and undefined religion before God and the Father is this: to visit orphans and widows in their trouble, and to keep oneself unspotted from the world." James 1:27

Those who have an ear to hear! Get rid of the bond woman and her son out of thy camp! The Lord says there are three types of people: The first is you who rejoice in truth and living in Him: The remnant. You love this Word. The second one is someone who, on accident, reads this, doesn't believe the Word and doesn't care, the heathen. Thirdly, this word angers you, and you are saying, "Who does he think he is?" If that is you, then this is for you. We love you.

{ SNAKE BITES }

"I see all. I know all! I am sifting, purging and revealing hearts. You lack vision, and many among you are spiritually sick because you do not discern the Lord's body."

I had a dream, and in my dream, I saw snakes hanging from my back. I started ripping them off. Judgment starts in the house of God. God is bringing glory to His house. Right now, He is cleaning house once again. Here is the interpretation of the dream that I had: backbiting, gossip, tale-bearing, lies. Snake represents lies being spoken behind backs of His people, bringing division and disunity. God hates this: lying tongues, those who sow discord among the brethren.

"For I fear, lest, when I come, I shall not find you such as I would, and that I shall be found unto you such as ye would not: lest there be debates, envying, wraths, strives, backbiting, whisperings, swellings, tumults." 2 Corinthians 12:20

Then, I heard the words, "A brood of vipers."

"O generation of vipers, how can ye, being evil, speak good things? for out of the abundance of the heart the mouth speaketh. A good man out of the good treasure of the heart bringeth forth good things: and an evil man out of the evil treasure bringeth forth evil things. But I say unto you, That every idle word that men shall speak, they shall give account thereof in the day of judgment. For by thy words thou shalt

be justified, and by thy words thou shalt be condemned." Matthew 12:34

Those who have an ear to hear, hear what the spirit is saying to the church. Then the Lord brought the meaning about brood, a group of vipers. Jesus and John the Baptist would speak and witness about it as well. These religious groups or sects were so engulfed in their pride and arrogance. No matter even after the vindication, not guilty. Even after the Word of God stifles their ears, there is no place for repentance in their hearts. Pride of being right, always defending your stand. The woman caught in adultery was just the bait that they were waiting for. They said, "We will catch Him now." Their target was not about the woman and her sin. It was the anointing they hated. Christ in you. Time after time, God would vindicate, justify, and condone the actions of His priest, prophet, and messenger, and most of all, His son. Their relentless pursuit became a satanic assault. Every time, they would disperse and come back together and try to find fault in Him. It was the Truth He carried that Satan was after. Make sure we know whose team we are on. From the pit to the palace, Joseph was betrayed by His brothers. From the cross to the throne, Jesus was betrayed by His brothers and His heritage. They hated Him without a cause. Beware of satanic snares, that you don't let Satan use your heart. Guard your heart! Whispering, back biting, and so on. Jesus called them a brood of vipers. God says, "This is happening at a high level." Everyone with their little facebook pulpit. Texting assaults. God sees all. He said this: "You better stop because the glory is coming and judgment is at the door. Love mercy, do justice, strive to live in peace." Then He showed me those who lack discernment for God's government and for His people. They will be exposed and must be humbled. This is out of control, and God gave me this verse:

"They are all gone out of the way, they are together become unprofitable; there is none that doeth good, no, not one. Their throat is an open sepulchre; with their tongues they have used deceit; the poison of asps is under their lips: Whose mouth is full of cursing and bitterness: Their feet are swift to shed blood: Destruction and misery are in their ways: And the way of peace have they not known: There is no fear of God before their eyes." Romans 3:12-18

It's time to love Jesus and His body. It's time to put away all jealousy, strife and division. You try and love someone around the corner, religious love, and you hate your brethren. Pride will destroy and overtake the one who exalts Himself above God's word. Evaluate your behavior. Love one another. If you are not capable of forgiving and submitting to the Word, you will not make it when the real enemy comes. I leave you with this:

"If a man say, I love God, and hateth his brother, he is a liar: for he that loveth not his brother whom he hath seen, how can he love God whom he hath not seen? And this commandment have we from him, That he who loveth God love his brother also." 1 John 4:20-21.

Always talking about love. Always misunderstanding what real love is. Love your Body because it's you. It is the body of Christ. Many false brethren will be exposed because of the test of love. As man thinks in His heart so is he. Jesus commands to love your neighbor as yourself. If your neighbor is in Christ then it's you! This is why many are spiritually sick because you have not discerned the Lord's body.

IT'S ALL ABOUT THE HEART

Cain and Abel: two brothers from the beginning, both with the same chances for acceptance.

"And in process of time it came to pass, that Cain brought of the fruit of the ground an offering unto the LORD. And Abel, he also brought of the firstlings of his flock and of the fat thereof. And the LORD had respect unto Abel and to his offering: But unto Cain and to his offering he had not respect. And Cain was very wroth, and his countenance fell. And the LORD said unto Cain, Why art thou wroth? and why is thy countenance fallen? If thou doest well, shalt thou not be accepted? and if thou doest not well, sin lieth at the door. And unto thee shall be his desire, and thou shalt rule over him.8 And Cain talked with Abel his brother: and it came to pass, when they were in the field, that Cain rose up against Abel his brother, and slew him." Genesis 4:3-8

In this chapter, we have two brothers. God said, in the process of time. How much time and what was God saying? "Cain, you're doing what you know you need to do, but you're doing it religiously." God said that Cain brought of the fruit of the ground. Was it his best? Was it left over? Had he already eaten, traded, and sold portions? God gave him the earth and everything he could grow. It's all about our hearts and putting God first in all we do!

Abel brought his first and his best with a cheerful heart, thankful. He was grateful to be able to do it. See, after the fall of Adam, God was still in communication with man.

God was not in man anymore. Even after Cain slew his brother, God talked to Cain. Cain tried to cover his sin, his shame, and his lies. It's all about the heart. Cain's heart condemned him, and his pride consumed him.

Don't let these preachers always tell you how much you're supposed to bring. It's not about money or the amount of it. It's about your heart to God. Man looks at the outer parts of man, but God always looks at your heart. The greedy servant will always preach to you about the amount of the sacrifice or about tipping God or how Cain spent and ate of his tithe. It's not about man or money. It's about your heart.

Abel, as soon as he set out to work for God, already had in his heart to bring his best to God as his sacrifice and offering. He was watching his firstlings.

God and pleasing God was on his heart the entire time. Was his motive the firstling?

That was just the manifestation of the heart. Cain was probably thinking of himself, what he was going to trade for and what he had. He lived by the law. He probably said to himself: "Oops, I almost forgot. I need to bring an offering. Here it is, God. Just like you told me that I had to do!" God brought the increase from the ground, but the only time

Cain had God on his mind was when he knew he had to do works. Religion vs. Relationship 101.

It's not about what we are doing for God. It's about how your heart is while you are doing it for Him. Remember: The Bible says, "Out of the heart flows the issues of life."

God is life. When God gets your heart, He has your life. Give him all your heart today. The Bible says: Believe in your heart that Jesus died for you (repentance is from the heart), then, secondly, confess with your mouth and you shall be saved.

We, as ministers, are under great misunderstanding. Some are training and being trained, thinking that if we can just convince someone to speak or say a prayer, "Jesus forgive me, come into my heart," and so on...that they are saved, but most of them turn around after they have prayed and go on living the same way. When the Bible says in **2 Corinthians 5:17: "Therefore if any man be in Christ, he is a new creature: old things are passed away; behold, all things are become new,"** they are not really accepted by God if they don't mean it with their whole hearts. They did not really give God their hearts. They need to know more that God loves them. All they have to do is to say something, but no. It's all about our hearts - knowing that you need to repent, that you are desperately in need for Him, that you are hungry and thirsty. You know that you need to turn from your old ways and change your heart - that's true salvation. David had a heart after God? Yes. He had some flesh/sin, but he had a heart after God. Here are a few things David spoke about the heart in Psalms.

"Be glad in the LORD, and rejoice, ye righteous: and shout for joy, all ye that are upright in heart." Psalm 32:11

"Shall not God search this out? for he knoweth the secrets of the heart." Psalms 44:21

"Create in me a clean heart, O God; and renew a right spirit within me." Psalms 51:10

"Trust in him at all times; ye people, pour out your heart before him: God is a refuge for us. Selah." Psalms 62:8

"I call to remembrance my song in the night: I commune with mine own heart: and my spirit made diligent search."

Psalms 77:6

"A froward heart shall depart from me: I will not know a wicked person." Psalms 101:4

These preachers should be concerned and should be focusing men and woman on their hearts. They wouldn't have to beg for money because when God has all their hearts, He will have all their money. They will not have to beg for money. If you beg for money, maybe you need to check your heart.

Everything is about the heart. We get our heart in line with God, and that's when the glory appears in our lives. Remember: Jesus spoke to the Pharisees, the religious leaders of that time.

"Thou blind Pharisee, cleanse first that which is within the cup and platter, that the outside of them may be clean also. Woe unto you, scribes and Pharisees, hypocrites! for ye are like unto whited sepulchers, which indeed appear beautiful outward, but are within full of dead men's bones, and of all uncleanness. Even so ye also outwardly appear righteous unto men, but within ye are full of hypocrisy and iniquity." Matthew 23:26-28

This is exactly why Jesus is saying: Works, religion, it's what's in the cup that matters. What is inside your heart, in your spirit? We must cleanse our hearts through repentance and have our minds on Him. If you are only seeking God on Sundays, just stay home because he said that it is better to be "cold or hot," not lukewarm Christians who only have God on their hearts once or twice a week. He is an everyday God. He has to always be on your mind. Then whatever comes out of you is accepted by Him: Your time, your finances, your family, your marriage, your ministry, everything. Then these are seeds sown that shall produce life. Then abundance comes.

God will not give to a goat what belongs to a sheep. Jesus spoke in Matthew about the heart.

"Blesseth are the pure in heart they shall see God." Matthew 5:8

"For where your treasure is so shall your heart be also." Matthew 6:21 "A good man out of the good treasure of his heart bring forth good things." Matthew 12:35

Jesus said in **Matthew 22:37, "Thou shall love your God with all your heart, all your soul, all your mind."** You see, Abel was loving God with all these but Cain only with his mind. For example: "It's time to give to God – here is what you commanded of me. It's Sunday, here is my offering." He had God on his mind but not on his heart. Jesus is saying: We have Cains and Abels in the church today. God puts it like this: "tares and wheat – sheep and goats." We must get back to the heart of it all. It's not about ministry. Not about money. It's about the heart. Ministry will come automatically with a right heart. Here is what Solomon – a man of wisdom – spoke about the heart:

"Heaviness in the heart of man maketh it stoop: but a good word maketh it glad." Proverbs 12:25

"The lips of the wise disperse knowledge: but the heart of the foolish doeth not so." Proverbs 15:7

"He that trusteth in his own heart is a fool: but whoso walketh wisely, he shall be delivered." Proverbs 28:26

"A merry heart maketh a cheerful countenance: but by sorrow of the heart the spirit is broken." Proverbs 15:13

"When he speaketh fair, believe him not: for there are seven abominations in his heart." Proverbs 26:25

The scriptures above are only a few, but God talks about the heart over seven hundred and thirty times in the

Bible. Jesus spoke in Mark when Isaiah prophesied of hypocrites, as it is written: "This people honors me with their lips but their hearts are far from me."

"He answered and said unto them, Well hath Esaias prophesied of you hypocrites, as it is written, This people honoureth me with their lips, but their heart is far from me. Howbeit in vain do they worship me, teaching for doctrines the commandments of men. For laying aside the commandment of God, ye hold the tradition of men, as the washing of pots and cups: and many other such like things ye do." Mark 7:7-8

Abel was righteous in his heart. Cain was religious in his heart. Steven even spoke about the heart to the religious.

"Ye stiff-necked and uncircumcised in heart and ears, ye do always resist the Holy Ghost: as your fathers did, so do ye."

Acts 7:51

Now God is still talking about the heart. God wants His church and their hearts. Let's give back our idols to Pharaoh. Let's give our hearts back to our Father. He promises to keep a smile on our face. Give to Caesar what is Caesar's. Give to God what is God's. God does not need your things. He desires your heart so he can give you things.

26

THE SHIFT IS ON

The shift is on! Attention, all saints! The move is to action. No longer will we build upon man's order. No longer will we say, "I am of Paul or I am of Cephus." No longer will God allow these ministers to conduct their ministries out of order. God is bringing his order over the globe for this set time. Mindsets must be broken; kingdom minds put on.

New mantles have been released on the body of Christ, and those who have an ear must hear what the Spirit is saying to the church. Big churches and ministries: Return to your first love. Repent - do the first works. You say you have need of nothing. You have become naked and blind in spirit. You have allowed the Jezebel harlot in. You release vision out of your own spirit. You lead the free back into captivity. You have not desired the new wine.

Church of God, return to Me. Release My people. I am now merging or marrying together the apostle and the prophet, a double mantle. These bones shall live. There is a remnant that has not bowed their knees to Baal. I am blessing those who have been set aside. I am calling you back together. Come out of the wilderness. Children of God, the Lord says, "You must not only be fed, but feed yourselves."

Much tainting of the word is all over. The blind are leading the blind. Don't depend on a name or a face. Seducing spirits are among us. Depend on the Holy Spirit. Many are under deception. Of course, they don't know it. Those who God has called to the apostolic must be prophetic and those who God has called to be a prophet will be apostolic. There is a changing. The Davids are taking their place. God is turning it around. Double mantles, prophetic apostles, apostolic prophets. We must hear from our spirit, not our minds. God has offices.

Don't listen to any that say that God has no prophets or that this is only for the Old Testament. We can all prophesy, but they don't understand the difference between a prophet and the gift of prophecy. They are babies and need to be taught.

We must be bold for the love of the Body. God is going to speak. God is breaking down the house of Dagon. He is breaking down the house of Esau. What you could do and get away with is now coming full circle.

God is releasing His bride from the hands of man. He is gathering His elect from the four winds. Jealousy has no place in His Body. You have been jealous of the new wine instead of getting your own.

There is a new church arising and quickly. The deaf will get deafer, the dumb will get dumber. So break off this deaf and dumb spirit. Repent and return to me. I am speaking through My apostles and prophets, not those prophets who are prostituting their gift for money and fame.

There is a supernatural release coming. Dormant seed is going to be multiplied. The seed that has been sown in the right ground, fertile ground, will be multiplied. Now is the time to sow. Hear carefully where God directs you to sow. He is cutting off finances to the rebellious.

Obedience is better than sacrifice. If signs and wonders are not following the Word, search, find out, pray for those leaders to repent. See where the tainting is. Test the spirits, protect yourself. This is a serious time and an exciting time. Don't be left behind. We shall speak the word of the Lord as He speaks. We obey. We love you and please search your hearts and hearken to the voice of God. Be free!

27

TABLETS OF FLESH

For the law is a shadow of what is to come and good things. The early sacrifice is done away with, but the law is not done away with--for now we have a better covenant but more laws, and these laws shall be written on the heart of man. We cannot go a year and then repent. We now have a harder covenant. Repent immediately. For if you continue to sin, you shall have a hard heart. The commandments given by Jesus aren't just sin. Get off your blessed assurance and go tell them. Heal them. Do the work of an evangelist. If you're not doing it, you are breaking a commandment. These grace preachers –they try to bring this new covenant--Bliss. "O, Jesus did it all on the cross," they say. Yes, He did, but receive Him. Then you get your turn to go and hang on that cross. In this sense, die to your desires. Be a doer of the Word and not a hearer only. You, foolish virgin, become wise. Keep yourself unspotted from the world. If you are a respecter of persons, you are in sin.

Then the law is still alive in you. We have more judgment because we now have the Holy Spirit here to be able to become holy and righteous. So, really, it was easier in the Old Testament because God knew that man could not live without sin, so, he receives a man of faith with sin into

Abraham's bosom until Jesus shed His blood for them. Don't tell me everyone had time to sacrifice an animal before they died? Come on. God received faithful men with hearts after him until Jesus took the blood, put it on the altar in heaven, and took the keys to hell, death, and the grave. Now, we have grace! Yes, grace to be saved, but after that you must daily sacrifice your animal, in other words, with your word of repentance, as soon as the Holy Spirit convicts you daily, hourly, minute by minute. The Truth sets you free and grace empowers you to stay free and to overcome.

"Then he said lo, I come to do thy will, O God. He takes away the first that He may establish the second. By which will we are sanctified through the offering of the body of Jesus Christ once and for all." Hebrews 10:9-10

Now we are our own high priest, and the veil is torn so we go boldly to God even though we have sinned. See, Brothers, you see certain kinds of sin bigger than others, so you tend to neglect little ones in your mind. Sin is sin to God. Jesus is our holiness and our righteousness. It is not by works anymore. When Holy Spirit convicts you of anything-- that is sin—no questions asked. Period. Stay away from these false teachers and heresies. They preach adulteress doctrines of devils, using the grace of God in vain. God calls them, "Reprobates."

"This *is* the covenant that I will make with them after those days, saith the Lord, I will put my laws into their hearts, and in their minds will I write them." Hebrews 10:16

228

Remember: Water is the word, and if you are sitting under an impure facet, a compromising facet, a faucet that does not bring a sword, you will set yourself up for a snare by the evil one.

"For if we sin willfully after that we have received the knowledge of the truth, there remaineth no more sacrifice for sins, but a certain fearful looking for of judgment and fiery indignation, which shall devour the adversaries. He that despised Moses' law died without mercy under two or three witnesses: Of how much sorer punishment, suppose ye, shall he be thought worthy, who hath trodden underfoot the Son of God, and hath counted the blood of the covenant, wherewith he was sanctified, an unholy thing, and hath done despite unto the Spirit of grace? For we know him that hath said, Vengeance *belonged* unto me, I will recompense, saith the Lord. And again, The Lord shall judge his people. *It is* a fearful thing to fall into the hands of the living God. But call to remembrance the former days, in which, after ye were illuminated, ye endured a great fight of afflictions; partly, whilst ye were made a gazing stock both by reproaches and afflictions; and partly, whilst ye became companions of them that were so used."

Hebrews 10:26–33

Some Christians have not been able to get off milk. Strong meat belongs to the mature brother. We still have pastors who are on milk and who are afraid to step forward to give a full meal. If the pastors don't grow, then we do not grow, and that body withers away. Spiritual fasting is not biblical. If your spirit is not fed then you spiritually die, then sheep go and jump fence really quickly. They eat off some good healthy grass, then they jump back a little, fed and refreshed. They act like everything is fine, but if you look in the spirit, you will see that these sheep are withering away. It all stems from much talking - preachers with many words but no substance. Sheep feel like they owe that ministry or man so they are afraid to get real food because they have been condemned and shackled by soul ties. We begin to put on grave clothes. We are under the control of man with these feelings. This is witchcraft from within the church, and God does not approve of it. Control will destroy your destiny. Churches are only talking about their own kingdom and not talking about how the Body is coming up under their leadership and becoming greater, brighter then themselves. That is the kingdom. It should be advancing. My calling is to open sheep's eyes to truth. The truth will set you free. I love every brother and sister in the body, but I cannot stand it when men and women control and manipulate God's children for their own kingdom. If you are not feeding the poor, clothing the naked, healing the sick, casting out devils, going to the orphan and widow--not just one or two of these but all--then you are out of order and there is a heart issue here. It does not matter how big your congregation is. If it is small then you do less of all these things, but you still do them all.

Then all of you be faithful in the little and God will bless your ministry. What ministries are doing is meeting once or twice a week. They talk the sheep out of their money just to pay for the pastor's house and car, but they never really grow. I have no problem with that, but what you are doing is building your own kingdom. They say, "Well, one day we will do more when we have more people." Sorry. That is not kingdom, and if it were not for grace, you would not even have a church. This is a warning to those who do this in these last days. Grace is being lifted and God will overthrow that place. There seems to be a way that seems right to a man but is wicked in the house of God. You have failed the test if you are doing this. Now God is not going to bless or increase you, and if you grow without God, you will have to keep it without God. God is saying these truths because the harvest is here and the laborers are few. I know that the Christians are not few. We are mighty in numbers, but few are those who are willing to lay down their lives for their brother. Come on, Church, wake up and see the truth. We have a small percentage of Christians holding up the entire kingdom. Our own brothers and sisters stab the one who is going forward in the back with their words. God gives me dreams almost every day so I cannot be tripped up by man. God takes me up in the spirit or shows me what's going on. I was in a place and God showed me through this dream the people around us who were laying down their lives for being faithful to a church, but behind closed doors they were talking, back-biting, speaking negative things about us. I'm talking about leaders in a church.

Remember: God does nothing before He reveals it to His seers or His prophets.

We need to grow up, Church. Walk in love. Fear Him. Love Him. Everything done in secret, He will reveal in the open. He's got our backs. We must know the truth and the truth will set us free. We must take our eyes off man. I don't care who this man may be. Keep your eyes on Jesus and be ready to give a word in season and out. God is looking for a warrior who will speak what he wants to say, bold as a lion. Fear of man has no place in the Kingdom of God. Be like Moses. He told Pharaoh, "Let my people go." John the Baptist said, "You adulterous snake, cheater", and yelled across the street in front of everyone. Jeremiah said, "You will be in yokes for rebellion to the king." Paul said, "You foolish Galatians, who has bewitched you?" How about our favorite one, Jesus? He said, "You blind guide, you hypocrites. You look good on the outside but inside you are dead. Get behind me, Satan."

Remember, Church, in Ecclesiastes, it says, "There is a time for everything." It is time for the church to wake up, get bold over the Devil, and sound the alarm in the church, maybe put some fire under some people's bottom sides. People are on their way to hell. We need the truth preached. "Those who are not on fire, shut down your church, and let my people go," says the Lord.

Every Sunday we go to church. We have made such a tradition out of it. This should be a place for celebration. God never called church to be a preaching center for one man--every week to go up front, talk about what God is doing or not doing, every week. Paul clearly said, "Prophesy one to another." Fellowship together, share testimonies. You, as a leader, think people want to hear you every week. Believe me, Man and Woman of God, you don't have enough in yourself to continue to feed the sheep.

The pulpit is not yours. This is not freedom. This is bondage. The pulpit is Christ's. He is the head of the Church. If He wants His arm up there that day, so be it; maybe His ear one day. God is crying out to release His people, His gifts. We must continue to be reformed, but some leaders have a pride issue or a fear issue. That's when the devil comes to destroy, to bring division. The people are not free, but we will say we are free here. Do some of them really think they are free? They don't know what freedom is.

If there are not miracle signs and wonders following you, then something is wrong. Check yourself: Either your theology is wrong or you are not free because where the spirit of the Lord is, there is freedom.

So my prayer for you and me is to seek God, to ask for change. Humble ourselves. Ask him to help and change our hearts. Ask him to make us leaders who are not afraid to confess our sin in front of our people. Let's judge ourselves so God does not have to judge us. Let's fast and pray and give the church back to God. It is His anyway, isn't it?

WOE TO WHO?

Woe to those who are turning the grace of God into one huge party and a show, who are cherry-picking the truth, turning the Gospel into a freak show. God is saying that He is going to expose this counterfeit spirit that has its foot in New Age. Test the spirits to see if they are of God. Contamination of the gospel is heresy. God is revealing this spirit that is turning the gospel into a freak show. The Book of Jude speaks of the last days: The church in correction. Today people are making the Gospel a big joke.

On the far left:
- Anything goes.
- The Gospel of the big party.
- Mocking righteousness.
- Dignitaries using the grace of God in vain.
- Taking scriptures out of context to produce false doctrines.

"Beloved, while I was very diligent to write to you concerning our common salvation, I found it necessary to write to you exhorting you to contend earnestly for the faith which was once for all delivered to the saints. For certain men have crept in unnoticed, who long ago were marked out for this condemnation, ungodly men, who turn the grace of our God into lewdness and deny the only Lord God and our Lord Jesus Christ." Jude 3-4

"Likewise also these filthy dreamers defile the flesh, despise dominion, and speak evil of dignities." Jude 1:8

On the far right:
- Legalism all around and within them.
- They are more concerned with the Sabbath than with the power of God and Jesus. For them, if we don't observe the Sabbath, we will go into damnation.
- They kill us and themselves with the letter.
- They bring us back into bondage by their own revelation of teaching.
- They take away from us the freedom of God and turn us back into bondage to laws and ordinances, saying anything that moves is the devil, having a form of godliness but denying the power of God.
- They love to confuse people with doctrines.

Along with these comes awesome truths and freedom. The wine He is pouring out is His truth. Jesus is our Sabbath. He is our rest. God is not saying or giving us a ticket to sin. He is giving us freedom and joy and peace. The far left has been tainted, taking a false doctrine of love, making a mockery out of truth and freedom in Christ. We cannot cherry-pick. We need to eat His flesh, drink His blood, move in power, love the sinner, and hate the sin. This apostasy will be magnified by the anointing. WOE TO YOU who pervert this Gospel of righteousness, love, joy, and freedom in the Holy Spirit, using the grace of God as a ticket to act like a fool! I've seen people even passing around baby Jesus, smoking it. Come on. Get understanding of the freedom of Christ. Cherry-pickers, come down off your ladder.

"I marvel that ye are so soon removed from him that called you into the grace of Christ unto another gospel: Which is not another; but there be some that trouble you, and would pervert the gospel of Christ. But though we, or an angel from heaven, preach any other gospel unto you than that which we have preached unto you, let him be accursed. As we said before, so say I now again, if any man preach any other gospel unto you than that ye have received, let him be accursed."

Galatians 1:6-9

"Wherefore the law was our schoolmaster to bring us unto Christ, that we might be justified by faith. But after that faith is come, we are no longer under a schoolmaster. For ye are all the children of God by faith in Christ Jesus." Galatians 3:24-26

The fullness of this gospel shall be preached. Without repentance, there is no kingdom of God. Salvation comes by preaching repentance, Christ crucified, and resurrection power. This Gospel must be preached cover to cover.

Legalist: Loose my people from your laws and your Pharisee and "sad-u-see" ways.

To the far left that pervert, mock dignities, and make the gospel a big party: WOE TO YOU! Now God will reveal New Age in the Body and out of the body, only God knows. You have stepped over the line. Come back to Him.

Come back to the narrow way where few will find it.

The far left and the far right have made the ones in the middle continually grieve; the enemy is bringing division. God is standing in the middle calling his people back to the fullness of the Gospel - No division, laying down your opinions and heresies. Drink this wine, and you shall see how the enemy has made a mockery out of Me.

Now is the time that God is saying: Enough is enough. Unity must come to be, or I will remove my candlestick from thee. The time is short - Come and separate yourselves unto me. Then you will see truth, freedom and liberty, not a strange fire that the counterfeiter has tricked for them. Wash your eyes with solvent, and you shall see the true glory and the gospel with His power and unity.

Note: Prophecy Received on December 13th, 2009

29

WOW & WOE

Wow and woe. Wow to those who know Him and obey Him. Woe to every evil worker of iniquity. Changing of captains, lieutenants, majors, some generals forced to retire, to those who have refused to shift into the new skins.

The rebellious will dwell in a dry land. This year is crucial for repentance from dead works. The old wine is being drunk with drunkards, the World. The rancid fermented wine, lukewarm, compromise, tradition, heresy, unholy, all unrighteous motives will be exposed. Those who have shifted or are seeking to move with God - those who have their swords sharp - will be ignited with a flame of fire, with the new wine of truth, with righteousness and joy in the Holy Ghost. God is raising up sharp, sharp swords in the land. He is raising up fearless soldiers of truth who will begin to see the difference between a house that is built on the sand and one that is built on the rock. The storms that are coming to this nation will be expected by those who know Him. They will be securely fastened, prepared, rooted and grounded in love, God's love. Many will have to run out of the houses built on the sand in fear for their lives. They will run to the houses on the rock where fire will consume them and revive them from the storms of compromise, rebellion, and false love. The ship of the nation of the United States of America is sinking. There are many holes in the framework. Water has been flooding this ship.

Men have been bailing it out, but the water is overtaking it to the point where man cannot handle keeping it afloat. It will begin to sink, and you will see it. The facade will be coming down. Many false prophets will be exposed. At the same time, His bride will be standing tall saying, "This is the way. Walk in it now." Sharp swords will arise. It will seem like the church has become a legalistic institution, but it is love. The grace of God will be greater than ever before. However, many have been convinced that God has changed, but He is the same yesterday, today, and forever. The biggest poison in the shift will be pride. Not being able to let go of their own kingdoms like a captain who goes down with the ship so shall they go down with their kingdoms made of golden idols and manmade works. They will do everything in their flesh to maintain what God has no longer ordained. Rebellion is witchcraft so God is removing witchcraft out from among His bride. The single-minded will see prayers being answered, increasing like never before.

At this same time, the glory of God is arising. God is delivering His people at a rapid pace, those on the threshing floor. Do not get distracted by the phone or the doorbell. The enemy is trying to distract us. God is starting to spark fire around the globe for the final awakening.

Some will speak criticism. Do not fall into that trap. The enemy will always come to kill, steal, and to destroy. God must have all the glory. Stay little in your own eyes. Financially, the faithful are about to receive a withdrawal from heaven. Double minds will continue to wonder why? Why? Why? Repent. Give to God what is God's, and He will give what He has promised. He never breaks covenant. If anyone is out of covenant with God, repent. Line up financially. Many have been sowing into a religious system where God has blown out the candle already. Many have been sowing from a misled compassion for people or sowing to bread snatchers using the system of religion in vain. Sow into the power and anointing of God.

Many have been depending on Uncle Sam or on big pockets in their congregations more than depending on the supernatural provision of a God who can put a coin in a fish's mouth. Repent and come into the faith and power of God. We are at **Matthew 6:33** - to be righteous is to be in right standing with the King. Many have been warned.

Exposure is imminent. Do not look to the natural as your source. It is an empty well borrowing from enemy sources. Break all alliances from a stimulus and beggar mentality. Stand on the ROCK. This system is evil and broken and bankrupt, being taken captive as slaves to an ungodly, anti-God, anti-truth, anti-love, anti-compassion, anti-loyal, anti-peace, anti-holy, anti-protection, anti-giving, anti-righteous, anti-Christ system! Everything looks okay by the media and false prophets, but it is a sinking ship. Get in line with kingdom policies. Get in rank, line up. Love will be overtaking you.

It will only be your best life if you are in Him. Apostasy is a slippery slope where many have convinced themselves or have been made to think that God is of their own making. God will show them the way to the floor of love. Woe to the money changers. The Lord is making a whip right now. Clean your house or the bridegroom will clean it for you!

Those connected to the vine will see the difference between those who are following signs and wonders and the ones who have signs and wonders following them. Look to the hills from where your redemption comes. Daddy is pouring out His grace, His love, and His compassion in buckets to the humble. He will begin to do a big thing in little things.

Always remember: Whom God is for, who can be against? It's time to step out of the natural and into the supernatural. Healing and miracles will begin to increase. Do not look to them. Keep your eyes on Jesus. Build no monuments. They bring death. Those who are in the Truth will have right standing and shall see the rain. God is raising up rain-makers.

Can you see it? Speak this over yourselves:
1) I will change.
2) I will walk in holiness.
3) I will drink the new wine.
4) I will not be rebellious.

5) God, do not let me go.

6) God, forgive me. Help me to change.

7) God, wash my eyes so I can see.

8) Jesus, shine your light and search me, the depth of my soul.

9) Jesus, cleanse me from all unrighteousness.

10) Make me a flame of fire for you, a sword sharp and new.

11) God, send me. I will go wherever you are.

I love you, and let's take 2011 steps towards the righteousness of God.

Note: Prophecy Received on December 28th, 2010

30

HERE COMES THE BRIDE

Here comes the bride, all dressed in white... Where is the groom? He is inside the bride and standing right beside her. Calling all saints to depart from iniquity and return to your first love. The anti-Christ is setting up His Kingdom for the final showdown where light overtakes darkness, where the saints come marching in total victory!

Twelve, the number of authority, the number of the apostolic, the number of the tribes of Israel, the number of the apostles, the number of government, the government of Jesus Christ, the chief commander, the One who is appointing, anointing, releasing the ones He has had in the cave in training and preparation, those being equipped for battle. A new breed is arising, the burning and shining ones, those who are set apart, coming out of the wilderness with the voice of triumph, with the voice of power, with a new sound following the rhythm of the lion, restoring the sons back to the fathers, exposing false doctrines in the church, exposing names, groups, and false prophets, those who are standing in inspection with their belts buckled and shined. Boot camp is over, but in full session. Goodbye, limousines. Goodbye, mansions. Goodbye, $3,000 suits. Goodbye, teachers teaching God's inheritance in a wrong way "to get themselves blessed." Goodbye, Babylon! Meet the Kingdom of God! True riches are being released on those who are willing to give up this life. As Saul's body is already decomposed, old wine is being exposed. David and His tabernacle are being resurrected. The new thing will be on display. The old thing will be made right again. Back to the basics: God's people are tired of religion, tired of being slaves to big ministries, tired of being manipulated by Jezebel and her false prophets, tired of hearing Eli, tired of going in circles, tired of being entertained, tired of being taught by the letter, by old winos, but are ready to move in the Spirit and are ready to be trained for war!

Forerunners are being released who are preaching the fullness of a gospel that was stolen by thieves and wolves and hirelings. Charlatans will be thrown to the wolves. Laid down lovers of the Anointed One being anointed, being ordained by the Holy Ghost, not by some dead religious organization or legalistic institution straining at gnats and swallowing camels.

Pastors starting to pastor, and not being dictators, submitting to the apostolic. Evangelists more than ever will start evangelizing the world and not evangelizing the church over and over. Teachers teaching God's beloved to be in character with Christ, to deny themselves, and to take up their cross. Prophets teaming up with their apostles. Prophets being the sword of the Lord and the rod when needed as well as the blessing and releasing of God's heart. The apostles setting order in the bride and in the church of God. Moving in signs and wonders more and more, taking authority over regions and nations. False apostles will be found liars and exposed as well. As the shaking is increasing, purity is arising. Truth is prevailing. Humility will be the key to total victory. Pastors will have a staff with a crook and will run after the one instead of playing number's games with advertizing and entertainment. True shepherds, not looking for a name and fame. Their eye will be on the pearls of great value as these offices start to truly be put in order. Then they will train the entire body in the nine gifts of the Spirit. Not false prophets of Baal training believers to prophecy for money, running around prostituting their gifts for their needs and their wants, manipulating sheep, but true believers prophesying on the streets, getting words of knowledge on their jobs, bringing the light in darkness, not running after a title but running after the lost. Armor bearers being let out of shackles from child slavery. Seeing true repentance preaching coming back to the Church.

The voice of the Father being heard by the sons. Eye solvent finally being put on their eyes. Those unequally yoked with unbelievers will be loosed in business and in the church. The poverty mentality being revealed in this nation. Those pastors and leaders who are focusing God's inheritance on stimulus's and pharaoh's charity and all their liberalism trying to taint the bride to be depending on the god of this world, manipulating gain by fear and not Jehovah Jirah. Cultural lines will be crossed. New wine is truth, power, boldness, repentance, persecution, supernatural invading the natural. The World will see the difference between an unbeliever and a believer, a Catholic and a

Christian, a harlot and a bride. Fear of man and their titles and their religiosity being vanished by righteousness. Unity will come year by year, masses coming out of denominations, old wine, joining the bride and the new wine. And man's kingdoms will be swallowed up by the earth and a bride arising.

A church without a building. A church without a hierarchy. A church without a dictator. A church with the love of the Father. Glowing garments full of oil lighting the way. The few, the humble, the bride. The body of Christ fitly joining together, taking her place, finding her space. A light on the hill being a lighthouse to the lost. Smashing the altars in the church, altars of Mammon, altars of fame, altars of Babylon, altars of Jezebel and Baal. The altars of sacrifice and true incense going up into His nostrils, a sweet savor to Him that paid the price, getting what He bought and deserves: All of His body.

The World will get darker, and the liberalism anti-Christ spirit will be pushing immoral laws, setting itself up, continuing to try to bring in the one government and one religion, one false god. Natural disasters will continue and increase. San Francisco and its perversion will quake. Sodom and Gomorrah will shake. Riots, anarchy, increasing in Europe and in the States. Secret coalitions in darkness, fueling the unrighteous, setting up its system. Russia, China, Iran, Syria, Egypt, and every enemy of freedom being empowered by man and its desires for power and evil under the command of the god of this world. Israel will take out its enemy and cancel its plans, setting back the attacks for some years. Muslims will be trying to invade the USA with their false doctrines and lies. Radicalism is true to any believer, meaning they are following the way with all their hearts whatever their religion or book says.

Fear will plague the unbelievers and reaction will come. The stock market will continue on its course of steady decline. Mass media will still be spewing lies, but through all this many will meet Christ Jesus the Lord. The dollar bill will continue to decline, not because it's bad, but because of the anti-Christ and his agenda and plans because waste and bad management are being done on purpose. Socialism and anti-Christ spirits are not going to back down. The policy of getting everything for nothing is the new way of life. Scams, schemes, and corruption are the American way now. Now morals are declining, and God's hands are removed.

All in time, we will shine. The bride will overtake the darkness in full time. Joy will fill our hearts, transforming people. Not a culture or a country, but a kingdom in darkness making war on evil. It's time. God says: "Pick your side or He will pick it for you!" Every secret sin must manifest in the light. Fall on the rock so the rock does not fall on you. God is in the perfecting business. Sons just like their Papa. Come on out! Come on in! So Christ can come out of you and His glory will fill the earth. His hope will invade the nations. Will you be that seed that falls to the ground and brings life? It's all in or all out. No more playing the harlot! His bride is coming...

Note: Prophecy Received on November 26th, 2011

31

RIDE THE WAVE

We have piped. We have harped. We have sung. But you didn't dance. You didn't lament! This year rebellion will be magnified. Those who have plotted against the Almighty shall be shaken. Financial crisis will leave panic on the streets, but the faithful will dwell in the house of the Lord. For the last five years, God has given us His grace to turn to righteousness, but He was being silent in the test. He spoke through a few, but many wanted His voice to come in big names. We were in a test, and as American Christians we failed, but God is God. All His plans are to deliver His people. Those who stood for God on the righteousness of Christ will find favor in the coming storm. They will be like Christ. They will be sleeping in peace because they knew His voice, and they have been following the lamb. They are those who have not drunk from the political pool of compromise and the abomination of man. They have followed the lamb wherever he has gone. Believers who have been rebellious will be tossed to and fro throughout the ship, and then they will finally repent. To the obedient will being given authority to speak to the wind, and the storm will be at their command. God has spoken. Many have been following peace, peace. These prophets have been brain washing their spirits, but God is not mocked.

"When the righteous are in authority, the people rejoice: but when the wicked beareth rule, the people mourn."

Proverbs 29:2

So we see a storm and Jesus sleeping. God will give peace, authority and joy to His remnant, the obedient in Him, but not to those who have not taken His full counsel. They have turned grace into lasciviousness so they will be forced out to Jesus for help. He will rebuke them but bring them to the other side using His governmental authority to those He has ordained, blessed, and called.

"Now it came to pass on a certain day, that he went into a ship with his disciples: and he said unto them, Let us go over unto the other side of the lake. And they launched forth. But as they sailed he fell asleep: and there came down a storm of wind on the lake; and they were filled with water, and were in jeopardy. And they came to him, and awoke him, saying, Master, master, we perish. Then he arose, and rebuked the wind and the raging of the water: and they ceased, and there was a calm. And he said unto them, Where is your faith? And they being afraid wondered, saying one to another, What

manner of man is this! for he commandeth even the winds and water, and they obey him." Luke 8:22-25

So let faith, hope, and love be your anchor. For the unbelieving, panic will begin to hit the atmosphere. The streets will be crowded, and every sand castle will eventually fall into the sea. There will be a spiritual tsunami, but the faithful will ride the wave on their boards of stability, truth, longsuffering, and humility! Understand. There is not a band aid big enough to cover the internal infection of sin and rebellion against Truth. Stay in the house with the blood on the doorpost. Ride the wave. Love your enemies. Bless those who curse you, and God will turn the hearts of the sons back to the Father as Elijah comes. For the Spirit and the bride say, "Come forth signs and wonders." Speak to the storm. You are the light on the hill. God is in control.

"Trust in the LORD with all thine heart; and lean not unto thine own understanding. In all thy ways acknowledge him, and he shall direct thy paths." Proverbs 3:5-6

God sits on the throne. He is the wind. He is the fire. He is the rain. Praise Him. Fear not. Begin to rule and reign! I have never seen the righteous forsaken or its seed begging for bread. If God be for you who can be against you! Amen!

Note: Prophecy Received on December 12, 2012

COMING OUT OF THE CHAMBERS

"I see you. I called you. I know you. You have been in a holy chamber being fashioned and formed. This conversion from the old into the new sometimes seems hard, and sometimes it is hard to breathe. Glimpses of glory! Keep feasting on me. It seems lonely at times, but I'm all around. In this season, do not forsake assembling together, not under denomination disasters, but in Me. Family of God! You know me by the Spirit. Cling to one another. My character is being imparted to you! You are standing - believing the words I have spoken over you. I am doing a great separation, leading my sheep away from all the wolves. Oh, you know them. They have been making merchandise of you (**2 Peter 2:3**).

I am removing you away from the false prophets who speak lies over you. Peace, peace, prophets not only on secular news but on God's T.V. stations, fame seekers, spewing lies. They ran, but I have not sent them, shooting stars. The only thing they are interested in is getting you to the Holy Land so they can make a grand off you, selling handkerchiefs and scarves and oil on a table. My true prophets are concerned in making you a Holy Land. They are in a cave. How many false words must be spoken to make one a false prophet? Imagine, Jeremiah, Isaiah, Ezekiel, Joel, Daniel saying something that was not true? Where would you be? I'm bringing you out of the harlot want-to-be. Transforming you into Me. My prophets are buying oil from Me, paying the price. Elijah, come forth! My messengers speak just like Me. I'm not a man that can lie. Gifts that I have given you are for you to edify one another. This is not a spokesman for me. My offices have been taken by the desire of flesh - those who desire to be famous and only want their picture on the cover of Charisma Magazine. I told you, and I'm telling you again that I have put a lying spirit in the mouth of these prophets who ran ahead of Me. Prophets of Baal. Church, get ready. Get ready."

I had a dream on December 8th, 2013. Lord gave me a dream and in this dream was a man named Oral Roberts quivering his lips in the fear of the Lord. He reached out his hand and said REVIVAL! What the prophets of old spoke about will be birthed 1000 days from now. I know I was not alone. I felt he was speaking to all – the called out remnant. In my spirit, immediately I thought of Ezekiel (Prophecy about the dry bones – Ezekiel 37). Then Joel's prophecy (**Joel 2:28-29**). I know God is doing amazing things, but there is a transforming awakening coming. Then I prayed and God showed me this man of God would put his hands on people and mighty things would happen. God said, "I will put my hands on my people, and they will do exploits, mighty works for Me! But it will not be a one man show, but many glory carriers all around the globe. One man will not get all the fame. Hand represents the body of Christ. Also, the book of Acts prayer (**Acts 4:30**) that God would stretch forth His hands and do signs and wonders. This will distract and counteract the persecution coming to believers. These bones shall live! Spirit is going to be poured out on all flesh! Life, reformation, and glory. Souls will be converted. Oh, America, land of the free! Well, that's what they say with their lips, but truth is this is diminishing just like Me to this nation. Church, you allowed this to happen, but my mercy will cover you. My blood is over your house, the temple not made by the hands of man. My children, take the land. Take the land. Take back My voice!"

I had a vision: I saw a facade, a pretty perfect picture. Everything so clean, in order, and just spectacular. Behind it were woodworms, termites, and rotted wood from mildew and darkness. The cover and the roof were being exposed. There were scaffolds and workers chalking, painting, patching so it looked great from a distance, but behind it were worms, the termites eating away the structure. The foundation was cracked and many voices of iniquity setting up its anti-Christ agendas, secret meetings, secret vows, secret lies, secret societies, giving their will over to my enemy, the father of lies himself. "Everything done in secret will be manifested by My light. Be of good cheer - you have overcome them. Fear not. I am with you. This is why you see. The spirit of Truth resides in thee. I will teach you even to love your enemy. But it seems so hard now - just rest in Me. I'm God. I will do it! So many will come to My light. This is My desire - that none perish. Be patient. Always remember who the real enemy is. Not the false prophet of

Baal, not the president. It is the spirit deceiving them away from me. No matter how hard it gets, my power only manifests through love. I will do this. I did it through Moses. I will do it through you. My power is above every power. Stand bold. Stand strong. Fight the good fight of faith. I'm with you. Pray without ceasing. This is the time that all the prophets of old long to be a part of, this generation, but I have chosen you...Beloved with dove's eyes...Don't let those that have been taken captive by the lust of the flesh, pride of life, and filthy lucre deter you from Me (**Titus 1:10-15**). They will lose it all and gain Me back. But you who have been found faithful, not found perfect (**I Tim 6:10**), but faithful, will inherit the earth. There is a transition coming. You who have come out of the World, you who hate the World and its systems and its ways, you are called blessed.

Warning: Do not allow self-righteousness or condemnation to come to others through you. There is no power in this. Love is what I am and love is what you must be. Abide in Me. You will see the nations shaking all around you, but you will be called blessed. The greater works than the World has ever seen - His Kingdom coming out of you!"

Note: Prophecy Received on December 25, 2013

H.O.T. CHAPTER
33

APOSTOLIC DECLARATION:
{ THIS IS MY ALLEGIANCE}

"I pledge my allegiance to the Kingdom of God. I break all other agreements or vows to any other. I'm in this World but not of it. I'm an ambassador of Christ. I will follow Christ and His commandments. I will eat from His table and no other. Faith, hope and love will be my anchor. Every precept in the Book of life will I follow. I will pursue justice for the weak. I will strive to live holy and pure. The Holy Spirit is my guide, my friend, my comforter. I will follow truth. Then will mercy and goodness follow me. I receive the light. I will carry the light. The light will keep my eyes single. This is my daily bread. This is my vow! I receive a kingdom that cannot be shaken. I stand in covenant to Jesus Christ: My Lord, my savior and my deliverer. I receive His precious blood. I take my vow as a vow unto God. I cast out fear or anything that exalts itself above God's Word. With this, nothing will separate me from my creator, the true living God. He is above every throne. I will bow only to Yahweh. I pledge to His banner. His banner over me is love. And to Him I pledge my allegiance."

Made in the USA
Columbia, SC
20 November 2018